THE MORAL ORDER OF A SUBURB

THE MORAL ORDER
OF A SUBURB

M. P. Baumgartner

OXFORD UNIVERSITY PRESS
New York   Oxford
1988

Oxford University Press

Oxford New York Toronto
Delhi Bombay Calcutta Madras Karachi
Petaling Jaya Singapore Hong Kong Tokyo
Nairobi Dar es Salaam Cape Town
Melbourne Auckland

and associated companies in
Berlin Ibadan

Copyright © 1988 by Oxford University Press, Inc.

Published by Oxford University Press, Inc.,
200 Madison Avenue, New York, New York 10016

Oxford is a registered trademark of Oxford University Press

Library of Congress Cataloging-in-Publication Data
Baumgartner, M. P.
    The moral order of a suburb / by M. P. Baumgartner.
        p. cm.
    Bibliography: p.
    Includes index.
    ISBN 0-19-505413-X
    1. Suburbs—New York (N.Y.)—Case studies
    2. Conflict management—New York (N.Y.)—Case studies
    3. Suburban life—New York (N.Y.)—Case studies
    4. Neighborhood—New York (N.Y.)—Case studies
    I. Title.
HT351.B38 1988
307.7'4'097471—dc 19   88-5145 CIP

We gratefully acknowledge permission to include in this book passages
that were first published in somewhat different form:

"Law and the Middle Class: Evidence from a Suburban Town," *Law and
Human Behavior*, Volume 9, Number 1, March 1985, pp. 3-24.

"Social Control in Suburbia," *Toward a General Theory of Social Control:
Volume 2, Selected Problems*, ed. Donald Black, Academic Press, 1984,
pp. 79-103.

9 8 7 6 5 4 3 2 1

Printed in the United States of America
on acid-free paper

Preface

This is a study of how people in an American suburb manage their conflicts. It is the result of twelve months spent in a single town, observing, questioning, and conversing with the individuals who live there. At the very beginning of the project, several townspeople voiced doubts, wondering what of any value could be learned in their community about conflict. One remarked that the setting was "just a quiet little town"; another stated that it was "a boring place to look at conflict" since "nothing ever happens" in it. A few people were surprised the investigation was not taking place in a city. "You could find some good conflicts there," one person noted. Intermingled in these comments seemed pride at the peace which prevailed in the town, along with some regret that the community might appear uninteresting and insignificant to outsiders.

In fact, as the study progressed, it became apparent that open conflict in the town was indeed rare. The suburbanites studied were handling their grievances and disagreements in ways that systematically undermined confrontation of all kinds, producing a moral order noteworthy for its restraint. They were tolerating offenses and avoiding offenders, while shunning physical aggression and courtroom challenges. To this extent, the skeptical residents were accurate in their assessment of conflict in the town.

They were very wrong, however, to think that the absence of confrontation in their community makes them uninteresting subjects of sociological study. To the contrary, a system of social control that relies primarily on the tolerance of offenses, avoidance of troublesome people, and comparable tactics, making little use of violence or formal settlement procedures, is of great significance both theoretically and practically. Discovering the factors that create and sustain nonconfrontation of this sort can shed light not only on the conditions that promote tolerance and avoidance but also, by implication, on those that undermine quarreling, violence, mediation, adjudication, and a host of other sequels to disapproved acts. This knowledge, in turn, can facilitate efforts to increase or decrease these practices. More generally, given how precarious peace has proven to be in the human experience, it is of great interest to consider a community where peace prevails spontaneously, and does so with little reliance on armed vigilance or third-party intervention.

In light of these issues, the immediate purpose of this book is twofold. First, it is an effort to describe the suburban moral order in some detail, showing how a system of restraint and nonconfrontation actually operates on a day-by-day basis. Second, and more important, it is an attempt to explain such a system by specifying the social conditions that give rise to it. The book also strives to fill in a few pieces of a larger puzzle—that of how people in all settings choose to respond to the wrongdoing of their fellows, by whatever means. In other words, this study is meant to be a contribution—however small—to the general theory of social control.[1] It would certainly shock the doubting members of the town to learn that their behavior could have implications for a global theory that ultimately addressed such topics as revenge killings, witchcraft accusations, and litigiousness. There is nonetheless continuity and connection among all the various ways in which people seek to maintain moral order, and it is the premise of this book that careful consideration of one part of the larger picture can further an understanding of the whole.

New Brunswick, New Jersey   M.P.B.
June 1988

Acknowledgments

During the years leading up to this book, I have incurred many debts to people and institutions who helped along the way. I owe the most to Donald Black, who worked closely with me at every stage of this project, from the study design to the editing of the manuscript. His invaluable assistance has made this a much better book. Other people who read earlier drafts and were kind enough to comment include Valerie Aubry, Joan Bossert, Mark Cooney, Kai Erikson, Allan V. Horwitz, Scott Lenz, Stanton Wheeler, and an anonymous reviewer. I have also benefitted from the suggestions of Daniel McGillis, Sally Engle Merry, Alden Miller, Calvin Morrill, Lloyd Ohlin, Frank Romo, Thomas Rudel, and Susan Silbey.

While conducting the field research on which this book is based, I was fortunate to receive financial support from the Graduate School of Arts and Sciences of Yale University. Later, the Center for Criminal Justice at Harvard Law School, the Department of Sociology and Anthropology at Seton Hall University, and the Department of Sociology at Rutgers University provided institutional support for the project. Kathleen Keeffe, Susan Flood, and Toni Gould helped by typing various drafts of the manuscript.

Finally, I owe much appreciation and gratitude to the people of the suburb I studied. In order that their privacy be preserved, it is necessary that they remain anonymous and that their town be known here only by a pseudonym. These people—ordinary citizens and officials alike—inconvenienced themselves in many ways to further this research. They were generous with their time and open with their information. Beyond this, their intellectual interest in the problems of the study stimulated them to advance numerous analytical and interpretive remarks about the issues under investigation. They thus proved to be colleagues as well as subjects, and it was a pleasure to work with them.

Contents

THE MORAL ORDER OF A SUBURB

1

Introduction

This book seeks to advance the sociological understanding of conflict and its management by examining how people in a single community respond to conduct they find objectionable. The setting of the investigation is a suburb in modern America. At issue is the handling of interpersonal tensions in everyday life as these occur in families, neighborhoods, and public places. The central theme is that the moral order of the suburb is the product of a distinctive social environment—one, moreover, which is becoming increasingly prevalent in the modern world.

Perhaps the most striking feature of conflict in suburbia is its rarity. Grievances arise, but people contain them and confrontation is uncommon. Instead, tolerance, avoidance, and restraint in the pursuit of justice are much in evidence. A kind of moral minimalism pervades the suburbs, in which people prefer the least extreme reactions to offenses and are reluctant to exercise any social control against one another at all. A result is the widespread tranquillity so often noted in suburbia.

This book contends that such a peaceable way of life arises from fluidity in social relations, a lack of social integration, and relative indifference among people—all of which are customarily viewed as sources of disorder and antagonism in human affairs. Instead, as they occur in the suburbs, these conditions actually foster a moral order largely devoid of violence and rancor and noteworthy for civility and forbearance. It thus appears that the spontaneous peace of the suburbs, so striking in contrast to the recurrent episodes of extreme aggression and prolonged struggle that have occurred throughout human history, is very much a by-product of the conditions of modern life. At the same time, the disorder and contention often perceived as typical of industrialized societies are absent from the suburbs. All of this is particularly significant because suburbs are not marginal or isolated places, but rather increasingly central locations in the contemporary world.

Theoretical Context

In describing moral order, this investigation addresses issues that have concerned social observers for centuries. Early thinkers—Thomas Hobbes, John Locke, and Jean-Jacques Rousseau, for example—were preoccupied with the question of how human societies manage to prevent and neutralize destructive behavior by their members—that is, with how social order itself is possible and with what techniques are necessary to maintain it.[1] Subsequent work by classical sociologists, such as Emile Durkheim, Karl Marx, and Max Weber, also considered the patterns by which people exert social control against one another. Thus, Durkheim developed the thesis that the definition of wrongdoing and the attempt to cope with it are important elements of all societies, simultaneously reflecting and reinforcing the solidarity of collective life.[2] Marx and his collaborator Friedrich Engels advanced a view of moral systems as outgrowths of competition and conflict: Such systems emerge within specific social locations and rise and fall with the number and prominence of their adherents; they advance the interests of some but not necessarily all; and they generally impose different standards and different treatment on people of different economic background.[3] To these insights Weber added, among other things, a clarification of the forms and effects of decisionmaking procedures in systems of social control, particularly law.[4]

In the years since this classic work, a substantial literature has grown up around the subjects of conflict and social control. Consisting of numerous studies that are usually less general in scope than those of the early theorists, it has been primarily concerned with two subjects: (1) day-to-day social control in tribal and other traditional settings, and (2) formal mechanisms of social control—especially law—in modern societies. Devoted to the first topic are countless anthropological studies detailing strategies of conflict management such as vengeance and mediation in preindustrial communities around the world.[5] Addressed to the second are the many studies—by sociologists, political scientists, lawyers, and others—of modern law and, more recently, of experimental programs designed to provide an alternative to it.[6] All of this scholarship has yielded a great many empirical findings and has provided the basis for important efforts of a theoretical nature.[7]

Nonetheless, as a result of this polarization of attention between informal control patterns in traditional settings and formal ones in modern settings, relatively little has been learned about informal modes of conflict management in modern life. Literature on this problem has only recently begun to accumulate.[8] Since there is every reason to believe that people manage most of their interpersonal problems without recourse to formal agencies, this omission means that comparatively little is known about the moral order that prevails under the distinctive conditions of everyday life in industrialized societies. This is not merely a descriptive lapse, but one that affects the scope and quality of the evidence on which theoretical generalizations can be made as well as the information available to people who might wish to help prevent or resolve conflict in the modern world.

To explore the entire range of social control within industrialized society, social scientists must ultimately employ a variety of research tactics in a diversity of settings. Modern life is not monolithic but divided into numerous enclaves and subcultures defined by occupations, social classes, ethnicities, lifestyles, organizational memberships, age groups, and many other factors. Each sector provides opportunities for research that may yield insights of potential relevance to a general theory of conflict. For several reasons, however, the moral order of the suburb is an especially important subject.

The Significance of Suburbia

Lying outside the central cities of metropolitan areas in the United
States are numerous smaller communities collectively known as
suburbia. More Americans live there than anywhere else, and those
who do are disproportionately drawn from the ranks of the affluent
and powerful. For its residents, suburbia provides an environment
with a distinctive social morphology—that is, with a distinctive
pattern of interpersonal association. All of these facts impart a
special significance to everything that transpires in suburbs.

The Extent of Suburbia

The 1970 census of the American population revealed a turning
point in the distribution of people which had been projected for
some time: It showed that in that year more people had come to
live in suburbs than in central cities or rural districts. During the
decade of the 1970s, suburbs grew by another 17.4 percent, while
the population of central cities declined.[9] By 1980, about
45 percent of the American public lived in suburbs, compared with
30 percent in cities and 25 percent in remaining areas.[10] All of this
takes on added meaning in light of the comparatively high growth
rate that characterizes suburban areas. Although some observers
have begun to predict an end to the disproportionate expansion of
suburbs and even increased remigration to central cities,[11] thus far
the trend has been consistently in the direction of increased decen-
tralization of metropolitan areas. As a result, it is likely that in the
very near future the majority of Americans will live in suburbs.[12]
    The shift in population which has already made suburbia the
modal residence of Americans has meant that suburbs now contain
the largest pool of voters nationally and in many states.[13] Beyond
this, the population trend has been accompanied by corresponding
economic trends of considerable import. New construction, for
example, occurs in suburban areas at much higher rates than
elsewhere. There has been a relocation of many existing manufac-
turing concerns from the city outward, and new businesses appear
especially often in suburbs. Service and retail industries have also
followed the population in its drift. Thus far, only financial offices

have remained in cities, and they too seem to be starting to disperse throughout metropolitan areas more broadly.[14]

All of this means that, as trends continue, suburbia is ever more central to life in modern America—residentially, politically, and economically as well as in other ways.[15] One observer has remarked that "suburbia overwhelmingly dominates the course of economic and social life in the America of the 1980s."[16] As a result, the standards to which those who live in the suburbs are held, and the mechanisms whereby social control is exerted among them, are already the most widely diffused in the nation—and, what is more, they are likely to extend their jurisdiction in the future. An investigation of day-to-day social control in a suburban location, then, is capable of revealing the moral order most characteristic of modern society.

The Status of Suburbanites

The scholarly literature on social control contains comparatively little information about how people of high status handle conflicts with each other. Instead, most of the empirical knowledge pertains to social control among egalitarian peoples in tribal societies (some of whom were subject populations under colonial regimes at the time of study) and, within stratified societies, to social control exerted against people of low status by those of their own or higher rank. Perhaps the reason that conflict management within dominant groups has not received much attention is that it has not seemed problematic to researchers largely recruited from and supported by these groups themselves, or because, in general, more powerful people are better able to screen their activities from scrutiny. In any event, information on day-to-day social control among higher-status people can provide a basis for comparison with what is known about other groups, allowing an assessment and possible refinement of existing theory.

Despite a tendency for the suburbs of younger, smaller cities to diverge from the larger pattern,[17] and despite specific exceptions elsewhere,[18] suburban towns generally contain disproportionately large numbers of relatively high status middle-class residents. When contrasted with other types of communities, whether urban or rural, suburbs are more likely to include persons with professional and managerial jobs, high incomes, and extensive educations. The inhabitants generally own their own homes, and few are unemployed. Indeed, suburbia provides the residence for the majority of high-status people in modern America.[19] Related to this fact is the relative absence of blacks and other disadvantaged minority groups in suburbs.[20]

Those who live in the suburbs are also likely to have high standing of another sort—they are likely to be respectable people who participate in socially approved institutions. Suburbanites are thus more likely than city residents to be married, to have children, and to live in two-parent primary households.[21] They more often participate in a church or synagogue,[22] and they tend to be active in clubs and service organizations.[23] This pattern is partly a function of age, for adults who live in suburbia are disproportionately in the prime of life (itself status-enhancing), at a time when such participation peaks in all communities. Partly it is related to other factors, including the middle-class status of suburbanites.

Overall, then, the suburbanite is more likely to be a highly placed member of the American mainstream, part of the dominant group at the heart of American society. Beyond this, many suburban residents who are not themselves of higher status live in or near communities where such people predominate, and so tend to absorb some middle-class standards and modes of conduct. In short, a study of suburbia provides knowledge about the daily lives of elite people—an understudied group.

Suburbia as a Social Habitat

In the broadest perspective, any human society not comprised of primitive nomads living off the land is unusual:

> For over 99 percent of [their history] humans lived in small nomadic groups without domesticated plants or animals. This hunting and gathering way of life is the only stable, persistent adaptation humans have ever achieved . . . . Humans can thus be said to be genetically adapted to a hunting and gathering way of life, a way of life characterized by small groups, low population densities, division of labor by sex, infanticide, and nomadism.[24]

More recently in evolutionary history, people in most societies have lived in small, intimate communities based upon agriculture and animal husbandry. Cities—with their scale, density, and impersonality—have been rare habitats for human beings, and suburbs rarer still.

Viewed in comparison with other environments, suburbia contains a distinctive pattern of social relationships. It resembles cities in some ways and smaller, more traditional communities in others, but overall it is not quite like either. On the one hand are such features of life in urban settings as transiency, atomization, and autonomy. Suburbs are physically and socially structured in ways that allow a great deal of privacy and separation, and it is not uncommon for people to know few of their fellow residents.[25] More important, suburban households often are separated by a great deal of social distance. High transiency rates truncate connections between them in time, for instance, so that associates are frequently people who have not known each other for long in the past and will not know each other for long in the future. It has been observed that many suburbanites, at least those employed by corporations, are "like vagabonds, with their homes periodically uprooted and transplanted."[26] This restricts the number of shared experiences, contacts, and knowledge among the inhabitants. In addition, even while they exist, most suburban relationships encompass only a few strands of people's lives. Such ties usually arise from residential proximity or common membership in an organization, and they are only rarely buttressed by shared employment, joint ownership of possessions, participation in a closed social network, or economic interdependence. Much about the lives of suburbanites is beyond the involvement of those around them, and few of these relationships are difficult to replace.[27] Even within their families, suburban people, like many in urban environments more generally, experience substantial independence and individuation. Overall, then, suburbia may be characterized as a place where comparatively "weak ties" to other people, rather than strong bonds of enduring and great attachment, typify social relationships.[28]

At the same time, some elements of suburban life are reminiscent of traditional communities. Thus, when compared with inner-city urbanites, people in suburbia are remarkably insulated from strangers. Social life is encapsulated for the most part within private homes and yards, and, to a lesser degree, within semiprivate locations such as schools. Street life is undeveloped, and people generally travel in the enclosed space of a private automobile. Neighbors, though not strongly linked by any standard, usually are able to recognize one another. Although its extent varies, casual neighborly interaction is more common in suburbs than in cities.[29] As a result of all this, suburbanites are able to monitor their environments closely, identifying those who do not belong and sheltering in the privacy made possible by freedom of association. Furthermore, when they do venture forth into public places, suburbanites are unlikely to encounter people very different from themselves anyway. Suburbs are strikingly homogeneous by urban standards, a feature of their social organization painstakingly maintained by a variety of techniques, including zoning laws.[30]

In sum, then, the social system of suburbia is distinctive. It combines transiency with homogeneity, and autonomy and independence with a relative absence of strangers. It entails a diffuse kind of interpersonal association, marked by considerable fluidity and distance in relationships. Such a pattern of social morphology has important consequences for the management of suburban conflict.

Moral Minimalism in the Suburbs

Unaware that their moral order is of sociological interest, people in suburbs continually cope with conduct they regard as improper. This book will show in some detail how residents of a single suburb react to grievances they experience in their everyday lives. The most striking feature of the social control found in this setting is its restrained and minimalistic character.

In practice, moral minimalism encompasses a variety of responses to interpersonal problems, all of which manifest an aversion to confrontation and conflict and a preference for spare, even weak strategies of social control. Thus, depending on the circumstances, these suburbanites tend to tolerate or do nothing at all about behavior they find disturbing, abandon matters in contention, simply avoid those who annoy them, approach offenders in a conciliatory fashion, or complain secretly to officials who might serve as their champions. Avoidance, in particular, is an especially prominent method of managing conflict, recurring in families, friendships, neighborhoods, and among strangers.[31] It is even possible to speak of the suburb as a culture of avoidance.

Avoidance—the curtailment of interaction with a person whose behavior is offensive—is a technique of conflict management that occurs in a variety of places.[32] It appears with particular prominence in the simplest of human societies, those of the so-called hunters and gatherers, among which it is "the most widely reported means of dealing with trouble."[33] Examples of societies in which avoidance has flourished include the Chenchu of India, the Hadza of Tanzania, the Pygmies of Zaire, and the Inuit, or Eskimos, of the Arctic.[34] In all these traditional settings, people use avoidance as a means of dealing with a diversity of problems, including homicide. Avoidance is associated in these places with geographic mobility, a low density of population, and a high degree of material independence. In making heavy use of avoidance, then, contemporary suburbanites have something in common with the most primitive human groups, however strange this might at first appear.

Moral minimalism is in large measure defined by what is *not* done when tensions arise. Anthropological, historical, and sociological research suggest that across the world two modes of conflict management are more prominent than avoidance and related tactics: *settlement* and *aggression*. One anthropologist speaks of these as "law and warfare" and, ignoring avoidance altogether, argues that every effort to cope with conflict can be subsumed into these two categories.[35] Both of these strategies are relatively undeveloped in suburbia, and it is largely as a result that the moral order there is so minimalistic. This is true because, where they do occur, settlement and aggression entail vastly more confrontation and rancor than avoidance does. Thus, settlement, which includes negotiation, mediation, arbitration, and adjudication, forces an airing of grievances and an admission of conflict between the parties. It may also require submission to the more or less coercive intervention of a third party to weigh arguments, give opinions, suggest future actions, and render judgments.[36] Aggression includes not only personal violence but assorted other punitive actions such as property destruction, deprivations, and humiliations. It generally fans the flames of hostility and tends to escalate conflict instead of ending it.

Although moral minimalism is widespread throughout the suburb described, it is not equally pronounced everywhere in the town. Confrontational responses to grievances—including criticisms, deprivations, occasional violence, and the resort to settlement agents—are more common among family members than neighbors, and among neighbors than strangers. Thus, it appears that more intimate settings foster more open and direct conflict management. Similarly, those segments of the population in which somewhat more cohesive and enduring ties are likely to be found are also those in which moral minimalism is least exaggerated. The town contains a minority of people who work in blue-collar occupations, and who, because they tend to move less frequently and to intermarry more often, are more intimate with one another than the rest of the residents are. It is among these working-class people that more confrontational modes of conflict management—especially violence and the use of the local court—are somewhat more likely to be found. Avoidance and other weaker modes of social control are especially middle-class phenomena.

In general, then, it appears that moral minimalism is most extensive where social interaction is most diffuse. Social density breeds social control; where the first is lowest, so is the second. Weak and fluid relationships foster moral minimalism in various ways. They reduce the incidence and intensity of conflict by distracting people from quarrels and lessening their salience. At the same time, since people in weak relationships acquire relatively little information about each other, the development of bad reputations that might call forth punishment is limited. Weak ties undermine hostile confrontations by depriving aggrieved individuals of supporters who might assist them in the exercise of violence, or whose presence is commonly crucial where negotiation and mediation flourish. They also reduce the role of informal third parties in conflict, for they involve a degree of social distance that makes people reluctant to intervene in the affairs of their fellows or to accept intervention by them. Beyond all of this, loose and fluid social interaction makes avoidance a simple matter: It is easy to end a relationship that hardly exists.

The high social status of suburbanites and the material equality and autonomy that prevail among them also appear to foster moral minimalism. High status discourages the airing of sensitive grievances before outsiders, except where people of even higher status are available to fill the role of third party. Since most suburban settings contain no clearly superordinate individuals to whom people can turn with their personal problems, the use of third parties is greatly restricted. This is true for mediators and counselors as well as for arbitrators and judges. To the extent that third-party settlement with its attendant confrontation is undermined, moral minimalism is encouraged. The effect of social status helps to account for some of the differences between working-class and middle-class strategies of conflict management.

As ensuing chapters consider these relationships in more detail, every effort is made to describe and analyze suburban social life with scientific detachment. This work is written in the spirit of traditional anthropology, in which the habits of unknown tribes have been discovered and recorded for future generations. Hence, no assumption is made of previous knowledge of suburbia, although many readers will have such knowledge. Nor are matters of evaluation addressed here. Some people might find in the moral order of the suburbs a highly civilized pattern of life, while others might react to it as cold, repressed, or even cowardly. No position on these questions is taken. Rather, the subject matter is treated as naturalistically as possible. It is hoped that the suburbia thus described emerges in the following pages as an intriguing social specimen, one with a moral order of great human as well as scientific significance.

2
The Town and the Study

This book presents observations about suburban moral life drawn from ethnographic research in a single community. No one town can possibly represent all of suburbia, nor lack special features distinguishing it from other places. Nonetheless, studying a single town provides a manageable way of gathering detailed information that can offer insights into a wider range of similar settings. The ethnographic method, which allows for the direct observation and unobtrusive study of conduct that people are likely to try to conceal under less intimate conditions, is an especially effective means of learning about sensitive topics such as conflict.

The Setting

The town that is the focus of this book will be called here by the pseudonym Hampton. Hampton is a suburb of New York City and, as such, is part of one of the largest and most developed metropolitan areas in the United States today. It is an outlying suburb located some distance from Manhattan. At the same time, it is also a suburb of another, smaller Eastern city to which it is closer geographically. The town covers four square miles and is inhabited by about 16,000 people. It is a place characterized physically by wide, tree-lined streets and spacious lawns among which are set houses representing an eclectic array of architectural styles. U.S. Census figures reveal that in these houses, on average, 3 persons share 7 rooms.

14

The community is not new but mature and settled, with a history dating to the early eighteenth century. At first it was an isolated small town, then a summer community for a handful of wealthy New Yorkers who built lavish country homes there. Successive waves of immigration from nearby cities transformed Hampton into a suburb during the present century. Typical of many suburbs, the town grew fastest in the 1920s and in the post-World War II period.

Using figures compiled during the U.S. Census of 1980 as well as personal observations, it is possible to describe the town's residents in a general way. Many are commuters. Approximately 40 percent of employed people work outside their home county, with a substantial portion of the rest working in other communities nearby. Hampton itself offers comparatively few employment opportunities, though this is likely to change somewhat with the planned construction of several corporate headquarters. About two-thirds of the men in the labor force are employed in upper-middle class jobs, working, for instance, as doctors, lawyers, engineers, architects, college professors, bankers, stockbrokers, and corporate executives—some of whom are high-ranking officers in major American corporations. Most of the remaining third hold working-class jobs as skilled laborers and craftsmen, operatives, and service workers of various kinds. A few people, largely of working-class origin, have opened small shops in town. Only a small portion of the men are engaged in traditional lower-middle class, white-collar jobs. The town is thus essentially polarized by male occupation into two social categories—the majority upper-middle class and the minority working class. There is little ambiguity about the place of most people in a class structure determined by mode of work, and in this study, class affiliation is defined by occupation: Upper-middle class people are those who live in households in which the men are professionals and managers, and working-class people are those whose male household heads engage in manual labor. In both populations, some married women work outside of the home, while many others are full-time housewives.

Because of the extent to which the families of Hampton cluster into two distinct status populations, summary statistics on income and education can be misleading. There is no "typical" town resident; separate figures on the middle class and the working class would give a truer picture of the community. When the 1980 census was taken, the average family income was $37,000 annually. Only 2.5 percent of the population was at the poverty level, and less than 1 percent received welfare assistance. The average level of education stood at several years of college. However, middle-class people as a group earn higher salaries than working-class people and are more affluent. (This is true even though many working-class people are quite well off financially, and a few have substantial real-estate holdings beyond their own homes.) A college education is the norm for middle-class people but is less common among working-class people.

Corresponding to a social-class division in the town is an ethnic one. Most middle-class people in Hampton are of Northern-European extraction—Anglo-Saxon, German, Scottish, French, Scandinavian, and Irish backgrounds are all represented. A small number are of Italian, Jewish, Polish, or other ancestry. Working-class people, on the other hand, are mostly Italian-Americans, members of an ethnic community founded by immigrants who worked as groundskeepers and maids on the estates of the wealthy one hundred years ago. The working-class population also includes a small black community with a history similar to that of the Italian-Americans, and a number of individuals of other backgrounds. Hence, although some Italian-Americans are members of the middle class and a substantial proportion of working-class people are not of Italian extraction, there is a considerable correlation between social class and ethnicity in the town.

Other things distinguish the two classes as well. In 1980 only slightly over half of all families had been living in their homes for at least five years, but middle-class people are more geographically mobile, and their pasts and futures in the town considerably shorter on average. They are also more atomized, since they are farther from members of their larger families and less integrated into cohesive, intimate neighborhood and friendship groups. Working-class people, on the other hand, change their residences less often and are more likely to be surrounded by relatives, friends, and associates assembled into enduring circles and networks.

At the same time, there are many similarities between the groups. Unemployment among men is exceptionally rare throughout the town, and home ownership the norm. The great majority of people live with their nuclear families in one-family, detached dwellings. Neighborhoods tend to be homogeneous, so that people of both social classes usually live near others like themselves. Direct ties of dependency between neighbors, however, are virtually nonexistent; each household is autonomous. Finally, while there are extremes of wealth in the town, most households from both social classes have outwardly quite similar consumption patterns, so that the suburban stereotype of a small family on its own piece of land, accumulating material possessions like those of its neighbors, is a reasonably accurate portrayal of Hampton's inhabitants.

On a day-to-day basis, the character of life in the town varies for different people—for a commuter compared to a full-time housewife, for example—but there are general tendencies that affect all residents. Hampton is a tidy place where people are attentive to the physical appearance of their property, so many hours are spent gardening, mowing the lawn, raking leaves, or fixing up household interiors. It is a quiet place with an undeveloped street life where people are relatively secluded and where leisure-time activities run to golf, jogging, impromptu ballgames, television, shopping, and bridge. People in the town have ample opportunity to attend classes on cooking, dance, or computer programming; to participate in service organizations and clubs; and to take advantage of local resources such as gourmet restaurants, public lectures, theatrical productions, and community recreational facilities. However, people are under little pressure to do any of these things, and individuals may be as withdrawn as they choose.

One feature of this setting which has special relevance is the diversity of social control mechanisms theoretically available to the population. People have the option of doing any of a number of things about their grievances, ranging from taking no action at all to engaging in violent self-help or initiating a legal proceeding. Between the extremes lie a large variety of possible tactics, including avoidance or abandonment, ridicule, negotiation, mediation (by family members, neighbors, friends, or clergy), recourse to psychiatric therapy, and complaints to elected officials (the mayor and six town council members), among others. The legal option is itself multifaceted, possibly involving the town's 30-man police force, the municipal criminal court (a lower criminal court empowered to resolve matters in which the maximum penalty is six months in jail or a $500 fine, and to hold preliminary hearings on more serious charges), the county civil court, or such local administrative agencies as the Zoning Office and the Board of Health. The Zoning Office, staffed by two men, is responsible for regulating land use in the town and, at the time of the study, also did the work of the building inspector. It handles complaints alleging the operation of businesses in residential areas, construction in violation of statutes or without building permits, conversion of space to rental units in contravention of rules specifying where apartments may be located, ownership of prohibited animals, and miscellaneous other offenses. The Board of Health, staffed for legal purposes by three sanitarians, is responsible for protecting citizens from potential health hazards. Besides complaints from tenants about housing-code violations and from customers about restaurants and food shops, the Board receives complaints alleging improper disposal of garbage, excessive noise or fumes, health menaces caused by pets, overgrown weeds, and similar problems. In practice, a person with a grievance can usually choose to proceed in any of several ways, and some choices are much more popular than others.

The Study

Research in Hampton took place over a period of twelve months in 1978 and 1979, and began with two questions. The first, strictly descriptive in nature, was: How do the suburbanites of Hampton define and manage their grievances against one another? The second and more difficult was: What in the social environment of the town explains reactions to behavior deemed unacceptable? In dealing with these issues, the study considered only the moral life of townspeople among themselves. Thus, conflicts in employment relations and consumer dealings—which commonly involve outsiders—do not figure in this account. The data instead describe social control arising in the course of strictly personal relationships between family members, friends, neighbors, and strangers.

The investigation proceeded through the complex of techniques known in social science as *participant observation*—primarily direct observation and informal interviewing. Information also came from written sources such as local newspapers and court records, and from formal interviews with various social-control specialists, including police officers, elected officials, the municipal judge and prosecutor, juvenile authorities, administrative officers, and members of the clergy. Overall, such methods seem especially suitable for learning about the sensitive topic of interpersonal conflict.[1] They do, however, involve certain costs, perhaps most important of which is the inability to assemble a random sample of disputes. Although it was possible to observe directly nearly all of the matters heard in the municipal court over many months, in a town as large as Hampton only a fraction of all conflicts could be uncovered. Like other field studies of conflict management, this one clearly yielded a somewhat disproportionate amount of information about dramatic disputes and sanctions.[2] The lack of a random sample makes it impossible to present quantitative summaries of the data. Nonetheless, since the cases in this study are drawn from all segments of the community and reflect input from a wide variety of sources, they should constitute a reasonably representative collection of conflicts and settlement strategies in Hampton.

The people who provided information were a diverse group: some were middle-class, some working-class; some were male, others female; some were adult, others adolescent. A few people offered a disproportionate amount of input, taking on the role of key informants. One family in particular generated a great deal of information, in part because they were members of the middle class with close ties to working-class individuals, had lived in the town for a long time, and included in their ranks an elected official and a municipal employee with wide exposure to the public. Insofar as the larger group of informants was skewed in any way, it tended to overrepresent middle-class individuals and to underrepresent members of the town's black population.

People interviewed informally were asked to describe any interpersonal tensions or conflicts of which they were aware. Conversations usually took place in private homes on an unscheduled basis with people who knew that a study of conflict management was underway. Overall, the town's residents seemed more forthcoming and uninhibited in discussing the problems of people other than themselves. Data generated in this way, along with those assembled through direct observation and formal interviewing, were numerous and of varied content. They were of three principal types: (1) detailed information about specific cases, including the identities of the principals, the underlying and immediate issues at stake, the measures of redress employed, and at least the short-term outcome of the matter; (2) fragmentary or incomplete descriptions of grievances, conflicts, and instances of social control; and (3) pertinent generalizations about patterns of disputing and social control made by townspeople, whether officials or ordinary citizens. Granting some ambiguity in distinguishing among categories, just over 200 detailed cases of conflict involving family members, friends, neighbors, and strangers were documented. There were many more fragmentary observations and generalizations by townspeople. The following chapters draw upon all three kinds of information, with greatest weight given to the evidence of detailed cases.

3

The Moral Order
of Families

Like most suburbs, Hampton is a community of families where
few people live alone or with those unrelated to them. Moreover,
people typically spend most of their time in the town in their own
homes. It is therefore not surprising that interpersonal tensions
arise more often between family members than between unrelated
people. For the most part, families handle these tensions in strikingly quiet ways that reflect a strong aversion to open conflict.
Moral minimalism pervades family life; restrained responses to
grievance are the norm, and people are reluctant to press their
cases against others forcefully. This contrasts with what can be
found in the domestic settings of many other communities, where
either violent confrontations or concerted settlement efforts are
sometimes considerably more common.

Conflict in Families

Throughout the town, similar sources of irritation lie at the heart
of a great many family conflicts. Most domestic annoyances arise
in the routine activities of everyday life rather than in dramatic
offenses of one person against another. Underlying the immediate

Part of this chapter was previously published as "Law and the Middle Class:
Evidence from a Suburban Town," which appeared in *Law and Human Behavior* 9
(March 1985), pp. 11-13, 15, 18, and 21-23.

causes of disputes, however, are the fundamental issues of inter-personal respect and obligation, individual autonomy, and control over material objects.

A few examples can illustrate the sorts of things that provoke domestic discord in Hampton. One dispute arose when a husband, who had stayed out late into the night drinking with friends, returned to find his wife asleep and his shirts unwashed. In another instance, a husband forgot his wife's birthday and stayed after work with friends in New York, missing several commuter trains before finally arriving home many hours late and drunk. In a third case, a wife became annoyed when her husband drank a Coke, something she pressured him not to do because of its high sugar content. A dispute between a high school student and his parents arose over a moped which the parents would not buy; another occurred when a teenaged girl refused to drink milk despite her mother's wishes. Quarrels between siblings broke out when a boy discovered that his brother had gone out of the house wearing one of his new shirts, when a teenager accused her sister of monopolizing the family car, and when two brothers disagreed about which television program to watch.

Whether or not people express their domestic grievances, thereby escalating their problems into conflicts,[1] depends greatly on the moral balance prevailing in the family at the time. Like entire communities or societies, families bestow "normative statuses" on their members;[2] a history of improper behavior lowers this status, while meritorious behavior raises it. Unlike the case in the town's less intimate settings, this status is exceptionally fluid in Hampton's families, continually changing in the course of daily interaction. Put another way, "normative mobility" is high in comparison to what is found in larger groups, where people know less about one another and encounter each other less frequently. Thus, a person's normative status vis-à-vis relatives is constantly shifting, and its level when a grievance arises predicts a great deal about what will follow. In general, the higher a person's normative status, the more tolerant others are.

When people do voice criticisms of family members, the responses are most often jokes, promises of future good behavior, or an immediate willingness to negotiate. In only a few instances do cases progress to real disputes in which offenders resist the claims of aggrieved parties.[3] Even when this happens, or perhaps especially when it does, the tenor of domestic social control in Hampton is remarkably restrained. Faced with open disagreement, relatives tend to react in ways that undermine and defuse hostilities.

Everyday Conflict Management

On a day-by-day basis, a few actions are used most often in the management of domestic disputes: depriving an opponent of favors, avoiding him or her, negotiating a settlement informally, submitting to the informal intervention of other family members, or simply dropping a conflict. Alone or in combination, they account for most of what occurs when two relatives quarrel with one another.

The most punitive sanction exercised within families on a routine basis (except where very young children are concerned) is the infliction of deprivations. This can range from the withdrawal of favors to some more forceful action, including one that amounts to the impounding of property or the deprivation of liberty. Simply withdrawing favors, the least confrontative version of this sanction, is the most common. In one case, a teenaged girl who had argued with her brother announced that she would no longer do his laundry or make his sandwiches. In another instance, a mother informed her daughter after an argument that she would not pick up the girl's clothes from a dry-cleaning establishment, although she had previously agreed to do so. A second mother punished her daughter by breaking a promise to buy her a formal gown for an upcoming high-school dance. In several cases, parents sanctioned their children by denying them the loan of their cars. Many spouses refused to run errands for one another or to perform services around the home (such as sewing or car-washing).

The more extreme forms of deprivation are limited, for the most part, to occasions when parents sanction their children. Since parents control more wealth and can dictate some of their children's movements (especially when they are very young), they have greater leverage in this regard than people in other family relationships.[4] On occasion, parents in Hampton have taken away their child's right to stay up late or to watch a favorite television program. They have impounded prized possessions, such as bicycles or baseball mitts, for a period of time. And, for what they see as serious offenses, they have punished their children with a kind of imprisonment, or deprivation of liberty, by ordering them to stay at home (except for "furloughs" to attend classes). This is known colloquially as "grounding" and was used, for example, in one case in which a junior-high school student brought home what his parents considered to be an exceptionally poor report card.

Deprivations—especially in the passive form of withholding favors—are not strikingly punitive when compared to the more violent options that people generally shun in their dealings with relatives. But other things that people in Hampton routinely do about domestic conflicts are even less confrontational and more reserved. Temporary avoidance, for example, is a very common response to domestic tension and helps to define the town's characteristic moral order. In practice, it may be more or less extreme, entailing some degree of suspension of normal interaction. It also varies in length, sometimes lasting only a few hours before a reconciliation occurs, other times persisting for months without interruption.

Temporary avoidance usually takes place while both parties continue to live in the same house. The two antagonists stop speaking to one another and curtail the amount of time they spend together. This strategy is at work in the following cases:

> The Morans are a middle-aged, middle-class couple who live alone. [Here and elsewhere all names are pseudonyms.] Mr. Moran works in New York's financial district, commuting daily by train. He leaves every morning at around 7:00 A.M. and returns home in the evening at about 6:00 P.M. Mrs. Moran is a full-time homemaker. For some years the Morans have quarrelled frequently, most often over Mr. Moran's drinking, which Mrs. Moran views as excessive. Another source of annoyance for Mrs. Moran is what she perceives as her husband's inattentiveness. Mr. Moran seems to have fewer problems with his spouse's behavior and initiates fewer arguments.
>
> After verbal altercations—or sometimes with just a new annoyance and no discussion—Mrs. Moran inaugurates a state of

avoidance. On one occasion, the couple persisted in this state for about six months. Mr. Moran went to work daily, while Mrs. Moran continued to care for the house. Mr. Moran deposited his checks in the couple's joint checking account, and his wife drew on them for household expenses as usual. She continued to prepare and serve meals which the couple ate together, silently. During their time together in the house, the pair exchanged no words and usually withdrew to separate rooms (each had a private bedroom). Each also maximized time outside the home during the evenings and on weekends; they went nowhere together. This state of affairs persisted until an adult child visiting from a distant residence learned the extent of the situation and successfully intervened.

Joe Bower, a youth of sixteen, believed that his middle-class parents were slighting his girlfriend. When he asked his mother to invite the girl to dinner, and she failed to do so, he began to avoid his parents. He would arise in the morning, leave for school without eating by 8:30 A.M., remain in school until 3:00 P.M., then stay with friends until it was time to go to bed at night. Sometimes he ate at friends' homes, sometimes at fast-food restaurants. Mr. and Mrs. Bower remained generally in touch with their son's whereabouts through their other teenaged children and did nothing about Joe's behavior. The situation persisted for a few weeks, after which the youth began to interact with his parents again as if nothing had happened.

In another case, a middle-aged government worker whose children were reaching adulthood became extremely upset when he learned that his wife was pregnant again. Blaming her for this, he slept on a couch and refused to speak to her for a week.

If tensions between two people arise frequently, one or both parties usually opt to exercise a modified version of avoidance on a routine basis. In such instances, people may continue to speak to one another despite making a great deal of effort to stay apart:

Sheila McCarthy, the teenaged daughter of a middle-class businessman, lived with her father and stepmother. (Her mother, who was divorced from her father, lived out of state.) The girl had wished to stay with her mother and claimed to dislike her stepmother very much. She engaged in frequent arguments with her. These were minimized to some extent, and hostility held in check, by a systematic strategy which Sheila practiced over a period of years. Simply, she made every effort to stay away from home as much as she possibly could without forcing an open confrontation. Thus, although she continued to speak to her stepmother and engaged in some activities with her, she was actually around her very little. After school let out at 3:00 P.M., she went to the home of friends or stayed at school to engage in a variety of extracurricular activities. Frequently, she ate dinner at friends' homes. Every evening she studied at the library until 9:00 P.M. and on weekends scheduled a full round of social events. When home, she holed up in her private bedroom with her door shut.

This *modus vivendi* persisted until Sheila, after another argument with her stepmother, left home altogether and moved in with a friend and the friend's parents. Her father at first did nothing about this, but when a few weeks had elapsed, attempted to coerce her return by threatening to have her expelled from Hampton High School as a nonresident of the town. He was unsuccessful; Sheila's host family succeeded in convincing her mother to move to Hampton, and Sheila took up residence with her. When the mother subsequently moved away, Sheila accompanied her and shortly after struck out on her own. She has not been in touch with her father since.

Modified avoidance of the sort that Sheila practiced for so long is quite common in Hampton's families, even though opportunities to leave one's home altogether for a few days or weeks are limited. Older children sometimes manage to stay away by arranging overnight visits with friends. When they do so, they may neglect to inform their parents of their whereabouts, but insist when located that they were "gonna call." A social worker in town refers to this as the "gonna call syndrome." As a rule, however, temporary avoidance is contained within the household, and outsiders—except perhaps very close friends—never become aware of it. This is as the participants wish. In fact, if faced with nonrelatives, disputing family members will often call a moratorium on their avoidance. One couple, who for some time have practiced limited avoidance in their home, appear together at social events and act as if they were happily married. When alone again with their children, they go their separate ways.

Besides avoidance, casual negotiation is a frequent response to domestic conflict. Like all negotiation, it occurs when two opposing parties "exchange information and opinion, engage in argument and discussion, and sooner or later propose offers and counteroffers relating to the issues in dispute between them, seeking an outcome acceptable to both sides."[5] In Hampton's families, this process tends to be extremely unstructured and informal, taking place whenever the parties are willing, wherever they happen to be. Furthermore, it is often brief:

> Mrs. Rosa and her teenaged daughter Linda, members of a middle-class family, quarrelled on and off about the amount of money the former gave the latter—Linda often found it insufficient—and the amount of housework Linda should perform. On one occasion, Linda was invited to attend a prom at Hampton High School and asked her mother for the money she needed to buy a formal gown. Mrs. Rosa refused and told her daughter to buy the gown herself with money she could save from babysitting. Linda became upset and accused her mother of failing to do things for her that other mothers did for their children. She began to avoid her mother, refusing to speak to her and spending most of her free time in her private bedroom or away from the house. She complained privately to her friends about her mother's selfishness and meanness. After a few days had gone by, Mrs. Rosa approached Linda with an offer. If Linda would agree to clean the bathrooms for several months, she would give her the money for the gown. The girl accepted the proposal.

In many cases, other family members intervene in domestic conflicts. The most common form this takes is friendly peacemaking, which occurs when someone "acts in the interests of both sides of a conflict and is, in effect, supportive of both without taking the side of either," striving "merely to bring an end to the dispute, outwardly at least, regardless of its causes or content."[6] They attempt to get the parties simply to drop their conflict. Also frequent during family disputes are efforts by relatives to mediate the quarrels of their kin, that is, to assist in the forging of a settlement. Intervention of both kinds—friendly peacemaking and mediation—is generally of a casual and spontaneous sort, and often people are unaware that it has occurred at all.

Family members who serve as peacemakers or mediators appear to be generally influential and successful in their roles. Their detailed knowledge of both parties makes their efforts more astute, and since they are intimates, they can negotiate from a strong position. Beyond this, they themselves have sanctions which they can employ against a party who refuses to cooperate with their efforts at achieving reconciliation.

Perhaps because families are small, even young children exercise an active peacekeeping role. Thus, in one family, an eight-year-old boy whose parents quarrelled frequently would, after an outburst, approach each separately to say how much he liked the other and how much he hoped they would stay together. An even younger girl interrupted many of her parents' arguments by bursting into tears whenever their conflicts grew heated. By the time children reach their teenage years, their techniques have become more sophisticated. Like adults who intervene in family disputes, they employ a wide range of methods to promote harmony. They may interrupt ongoing quarrels to dismiss the matter at issue, make a joke of the whole affair, or suggest a solution. They may listen separately to both sides, act as a go-between in presenting the position of each to the other, pass judgment on each person's conduct, and exhort or cajole the parties to put their disagreement behind them. Several of these techniques appear in the following account:

> Mr. and Mrs. Hauser, a middle-class couple, quarreled when the wife's attempts to get her husband to accompany her to a party were unsuccessful. After declining to attend the event several times, Mr. Hauser became annoyed at being asked repeatedly and accused his wife of nagging. An argument ensued, after which the couple began to avoid one another. Since both worked during the day, this was relatively simple; during the evening, each relaxed and watched television in separate rooms, then slipped into their common bedroom late at night while ignoring the other. The two prepared and ate meals separately. This lasted one day and into a second, at which time the couple's teenaged daughters intervened. They began to upbraid both parents for being "childish" and threatened to leave home for the weekend—though where they might have gone they never said—unless normality were restored. After several exchanges

with each parent separately, they pursued the matter when the two happened to be in the same room. By the evening of the second day, the parents were interacting amiably again, having decided to end their avoidance.

Adults similarly intervene in the quarrels of their children, or of their children with their spouses. Except where both parties are very young—in which case adults often threaten to punish each indiscriminately unless a dispute ends, regardless of the merits of their cause—this intervention too is usually supportive and conciliatory. When a mother argued with her 20-year-old son after she reprimanded him for coming home drunk one night, the husband succeeded in convincing each party to drop the matter. He pointed out to his wife that the boy might soon be living elsewhere and that she would then miss him.

For all combinations of disputants, family members routinely step forward to help heal conflicts—most times successfully, but sometimes not. For those residents of the town with extended kin nearby (usually members of the working class), intervention from beyond the nuclear household by grandparents, aunts, and uncles may occur. In all families, however, it is most frequent by those living in the home, where it is a standard feature of conflict management.

In the end, however, most disputes between family members do not ease when the issues in question are resolved, but when the parties simply drop their conflict and resume friendly interaction. They may end when one party decides to practice "unilateral peaceableness."[7] Grievances evaporate or are laid aside (at least for the time being); avoidance is terminated; disagreements are abandoned. This happens so abruptly in many instances that it greatly contributes to a climate of normative volatility in family life, in which states of peace and conflict are unstable and continually shifting. Sometimes dropping a conflict entails "giving up": After one couple had argued over the fact that the husband would not take a vacation with his wife, the wife decided not to press the matter further. Similarly, each of a series of intermittent quarrels between a father and son, arising over the father's efforts to convince the son to drop out of a rock band, ended with the father resigning himself to the situation for the time being. Sometimes brief apologies signal a party's desire to abandon a conflict; sometimes special favors are performed for an opponent. When they occur, symbolic gestures of this sort embellish what is otherwise a simple and anticlimatic process. With or without them, however, the result is the same: People resume their normal lives as if nothing had happened. Once open disagreements have occurred, it is difficult to imagine a less forceful outcome.

·   ·   ·

The responses just detailed comprise the standard repertoire of conflict-management techniques in most Hampton families, whether of the middle or working class. As a group, they are noteworthy for the extent to which they contain, defuse, or minimize conflict in ways that require little investment by the parties or other relatives. They are mostly nonconfrontational and nonpunitive. Overall social control in families is not only restrained in what transpires on a day-by-day basis, however, but also in what happens in exceptional cases of persistent grievances or simmering tensions. Two responses arising often under such circumstances—emotional distress and permanent avoidance—also reflect an aversion to open conflict.

Persistent Problems

Faced with persistent domestic tensions, people in Hampton generally continue to exercise their usual techniques of conflict management. Repeatedly, they will negotiate or submit to the mediation of family members. For indefinite periods, they will exercise modified avoidance. Even as quarrels become more and more frequent, they will do the same things they have always done, simply doing them more often. In a significant number of cases, however, people in Hampton engage in a few additional responses to persistent conflict or ongoing problems.

One means through which family members sometimes dramatize displeasure with each other, and bring further pressure to bear, is by exhibiting symptoms of emotional distress or personal maladjustment. As a reaction to grievances, this has some interesting and unusual features. Foremost among them is the way in which it sublimates and redefines conflict even while advancing it. Emotional distress is typically defined by all of the parties involved as the result of personality forces beyond the disturbed individual's control, and something for which he or she should not be held responsible. In most cases it is virtually impossible to tell whether the distressed person recognizes it as an expression of conflict or not. The ambiguity surrounding the intentions of those who engage in distressed behavior sets this apart from most other forms of social control and makes it extremely nonconfrontational in its own way. For present purposes, the exact motivation that accompanies distress is not made problematic. What is significant is that it occurs in the course of conflict, is responsive to the behavior of the adversary, and is capable of inflicting hardship.

Emotional distress can operate as a sanction in several ways. Aside from any guilt it may arouse, it inconveniences an offending relative to the extent that the disturbed person is unable to function normally and discharge obligations in the home. If extreme enough, it may result in the involvement of a psychiatrist or other professional, with the considerable expense this entails. In addition, it can embarrass and stigmatize other family members before a wider community of their friends and associates.

People in Hampton who exhibit signs of emotional distress during conflict usually do so in ways typical of "sick" or "crazy" people, as these are perceived in the town. Such individuals may fall into spells of listlessness and passivity, or of extreme agitation and flightiness. Often they are unable to cope with their daily responsibilities:

> Mrs. Swift, a middle-class woman, became extremely depressed after all of her grown-up children moved to other states—something she had not wanted them to do—and she was left alone with a frequently absent husband. Ultimately, she gave up her job and restricted most of her time to her house. Her only forays were to the homes of friends, where she made herself increasingly unwelcome by arriving unannounced and staying for long periods of time, saying little and looking extremely mournful. Her friends began to resort to hiding from her in their own homes, and also cut back on their formal

invitations to her. With the urging of her husband and friends, Mrs. Swift sought professional help for her depression. She was prescribed mood-altering drugs, but she took these only rarely. As his wife's symptoms persisted, Mr. Swift became increasingly concerned and rearranged his schedule to spend more time with her. After many months of severe depression, Mrs. Swift began to show improvement and gradually returned to normal.

A working-class woman became "nervous" because, she said, her house was "too much" for her. Among other symptoms, she would stay up late at night, pacing back and forth in her bedroom and running water in the bathroom. She was also irritable with her husband and children, and pulled the latter's hair. In a third case, a middle-aged working-class man said to be "unhappy at home" fell into a deep depression, sitting staring into space for hours at a time. A middle-class woman of Northern-European extraction became depressed when her daughter married an Italian-American man from a working-class home. All of this is consistent with findings from other studies which demonstrate that mentally ill people often have conflict-ridden relationships with relatives.[9]

Young people also exhibit symptoms of mental illness under some circumstances. Like adults, they may become socially withdrawn and listless, or nervous and agitated. Sometimes, young girls stop eating—a behavior clinically labeled "anorexia nervosa"—in a move that may be interpreted as a kind of hunger strike:

> Marilyn Stephens was a teenaged girl from a middle-class family at the time that her anorexia nervosa developed. There was much conflict in the Stephens' home at this period—Marilyn's sister was dating a black youth, which led to many scenes between this girl and her parents, and the parents themselves were not getting along and were planning a divorce. Marilyn wished the family to remain together and attempted to perform a peacekeeping role, but without notable success. Between her sophomore and junior years at Hampton High School, Marilyn began losing weight. At first she wanted to lose only 5 pounds, but she kept putting off the end of her diet and eventually had reduced to about 70 pounds. She also cut off her social life and became very withdrawn. Marilyn's parents, teachers, and friends were all very concerned about this. Her parents tried to force

her to eat, but were unable to do so. Finally, school authorities intervened and helped to arrange counseling for the girl. Mr. and Mrs. Stephens decided to stay together for Marilyn's sake, and peace once more prevailed in the home. Marilyn began eating normally again. She graduated from high school on schedule and moved away to attend college.

In another case, a young woman stopped eating, but continued to cook elaborate meals which she hid around her apartment and left to rot, an action her psychiatrist termed "punishment of her domineering mother."

Young people may also show distress or maladjustment through other means. Many—although of course not all—cases of adolescent drug use, promiscuity, petty criminal involvement, and failure at school or elsewhere arise during periods of ongoing tension. As a commentator on the situation in a Midwestern suburb has observed:

> Some children, deliberately or unconsciously, use academic failure as a weapon of retaliation against their parents. [They] quickly realize that they can strike back at their parents by flunking in school. The "Great Expectations Syndrome" [on the part of parents for their children] makes it easy to hurt the sources of authority.[10]

The same behavior seems to appear in other societies. One Japanese adult explained to an American reporter how adolescents in his country threaten to punish their parents if, for example, they are deprived of the opportunity to attend a rock concert:

> Ah, but the kids are the ones who control the situation. All parents want their children to study hard to get into the best universities. Kid say, "Give me money for Cheap Trick ticket, or I don't study for exams." Parent is helpless.[11]

In Hampton, this response is usually limited to poor performance in school and only rarely extends to "dropping out," a phenomenon associated with parent-child conflict in other places.[12] Along similar lines, juvenile delinquency in American suburbs has also been linked to high levels of hostility between parents and children.[13]

A few illustrations of these responses may clarify their use in Hampton:

> Diana Brady was one of four children from a middle-class family. When she was still of grammar-school age, her mother died; subsequently her father remarried. Along with other of her siblings, Diana disliked her stepmother very much and had frequent disagreements with her. Diana's high school years were thus characterized by much domestic tension and strained relations with both parents. Under these circumstances, Diana became, in the opinion of the adults who knew her, a very rebellious and troubled girl. She openly cultivated an active sex life, defying her parents by staying out overnight on many occasions and returning home only after others in the family were awake in the morning. On at least one occasion, she left a birth-control device on the side of the bathroom sink she shared with her parents. She also maintained an explicit diary of her exploits which she sometimes left out in a prominent place, where others might easily notice (and read) it. Efforts by her parents to criticize this behavior provoked heated arguments and no changes. Increasingly angry, Mr. and Mrs. Brady threatened to evict Diana from their home; in an effort to help maintain peace, her brothers took to hiding evidence of her activities from their parents. The situation only resolved itself when sometime after high school graduation, Diana took a job out of state and moved away. In the ensuing years, neither parent has received any communication at all from Diana.

A working-class girl began to use illegal drugs while in high school, because, as she said later when seeking therapy, her parents were "too strict." And a young boy from the working class who was on very bad terms with his father began to engage in vandalism and petty theft, something which enraged and humiliated the parent as a disgrace to the family name.

In a rare handful of cases, people go so far as to threaten or attempt suicide during periods of domestic conflict. According to town statistics, throughout the 1970s there were an average of two or three suicides per year—an annual rate consistent with the national figure of 15.0 per 100,000 people. Extensive information on some of these cases, and on unsuccessful attempts, makes it clear that in most of these instances the self-destructive behavior occurred as one move in a larger conflict with a family member.[14] One woman hanged herself after repeated efforts toward reconciliation with her estranged husband failed. Another woman killed herself and her five-year-old daughter by means of carbon-monoxide poisoning after a heated quarrel with her husband, whom she was already in the process of divorcing. And in a third example, a mildly retarded man living with his mother, a chronic invalid, unsuccessfully attempted suicide because, he said, he could not stand her any longer. Such unusually extreme versions of emotional distress embody in magnified form many of the dynamics common to every expression of this behavior.

One feature of emotional distress deserves special mention—the way in which it often involves outsiders in family troubles under circumstances far more acceptable than those usually associated with third-party intervention. Psychiatrists, social workers, doctors, and others who provide therapy to disturbed people are defined by all participants as help-givers interested only in the emotional health or social adjustment of their clients. Accepting their involvement does not entail a direct admission of interpersonal conflict, and it is not an open means of increasing social control. These features make it less objectionable to Hampton's residents than recourse to such admitted conflict-management specialists as the police or marriage counselors. It is considered improper to thwart a disturbed person's efforts to seek therapy, and in some cases, such as when a juvenile gets into trouble with the police for petty crimes, accepting the proffered intervention of counselors may be mandatory. Nonetheless, mental-health professionals actually do play a role in the process of conflict itself. They may certify that a person is in need of special attention in the home, specify conditions aggravating an emotional problem, and help set moral standards for the client as well as for other family members. In general, they bring an outsider's judgment to bear upon whether or not the disturbed person has a legitimate grievance and is justified in his or her response.[15] Beyond this, they may serve as unwitting means of punishment for an offending relative, if that person must bear the expense of their fees. Usually such costs are considerably in excess of standard court fines for domestic offenses that are defined as crimes.

All of this has much in common with the invocation of religious therapy for possessed people in other times and places. Plateau Tonga women in Zambia, for example, are subject to possession by spirits who demand expensive gifts and rituals as the price of releasing their victims; a prolonged period of disputing between husband and wife is likely to precede such possession.[16] Similarly, among the Somali pastoralists of the Horn of Africa, women with grievances against their husbands are prone to a troublesome spirit possession requiring the invocation of specialists to oversee costly curative ceremonies. The anthropologist who has studied this phenomenon concludes that possession and its cure comprise a significant means of conflict management for Somali women, who find many alternatives "blocked or culturally inappropriate."[17] In Hampton, people achieve similar results in analogous ways by exhibiting signs of emotional disturbance: They pursue their conflicts, but do not admit them.

The ultimate sanction exercised by family members against one another in Hampton is not emotional distress, however, but permanent avoidance. This takes the form of divorce when the conflict is between spouses, and of simple residential separation when it is between parents and children or between siblings. (Permanent avoidance generally becomes feasible only when young people have reached the age of legal adulthood, since before that parents are under legal obligation to provide for their children, and children in turn are legally bound to live with their parents.) In practice, people sometimes reconcile after initiating these extremes of avoidance, and they may maintain a measure of restricted interaction in any case, but generally both the projected length and extent of the avoidance is far beyond that seen in households on a more routine basis. People have decided that a relationship is untenable, at least in its present form, and that drastic action is necessary. But whereas in some settings aggrieved parties achieve permanent separation by resorting to the ultimate weapon of homicide, in Hampton they effectively just withdraw.

Much tension, built up over extended periods of time, virtually always precedes the initiation of permanent avoidance. In fact, most people in Hampton appear to continue in conflict-ridden family relationships indefinitely, simply resorting to the techniques of social control described previously. Some, however, finally opt for separation, influenced by any of a variety of circumstances. They may, for instance, yield to the counseling of intimate advisors, especially other family members, who have themselves concluded that separation is desirable. They may be spurred to action by the departure of a child or sibling who had previously performed an important mediative function—a factor frequently underlying the divorces of middle-aged couples whose children have just left home. Or, they may perceive some new misconduct of an offending relative as a "last straw" which makes that person "finally intolerable" and shows once and for all that the offender is incapable of ever engaging in rightful conduct—a perception also associated with much banishment in tribal societies.[18] Several of these factors can be seen in the following case:

> The Wilsons were a middle-class couple who had lived in Hampton for most of their married lives, raising four children there. All along, Mr. Wilson was prone to explosive criticisms of his wife and children. The latter perceived him as demanding and argumentative, and domestic life in the Wilson household was far from idyllic. Tensions and quarrels escalated sharply when the Wilson children became teenagers. As a result, the young people began to avoid their father, seeking to minimize contact with him in various ways. Mrs. Wilson, however, maintained her relationship with her husband because she felt it was best for the children in the long run. As the young people reached adulthood, they began to move away from home one by one. Several of them communicated to their mother that they wished to continue to see her, but only if they could do so without having to confront their father. This was weighing on Mrs. Wilson when, one day, a heated quarrel broke out between her husband and youngest child (who was still at home). Mrs. Wilson felt that the incident was entirely the fault of her husband, who was being unreasonable as usual, and it galvanized her to action. Looking ahead to a time when she would be living alone with difficult Mr. Wilson in a home her children would not visit, Mrs. Wilson decided on divorce.

In another case, a working-class woman whose parents strongly urged her to divorce her husband (whom they had never liked) eventually decided to take their advice. In several cases, a spouse decided upon permanent separation after forging a relationship with another, more compatible, man or woman. One couple divorced when the wife left for California with a close family friend, and another when the husband announced that he wanted to marry someone he had met at work. In a case uncommon in Hampton, a middle-aged man abandoned his wife to pursue relationships with other men and to work for Gay Liberation.

When permanent avoidance arises between parents and children, there is no official pronouncement analogous to a divorce decree. Nonetheless, many of the dynamics are similar, and the separation may be as absolute. In some cases, it is the child who initiates the avoidance by leaving home and severely restricting interaction with an offending parent; in other instances, it is the parent who evicts the child. In one unusually dramatic case, a white couple urged their teenaged daughter to end a relationship with a young black man. When she declined to do so, they forbade her to invite her boyfriend into their house, but the girl insisted on having him over, and he persisted in coming. Finally, one evening when both young people were together in the house, the father confronted them and ordered the youth to leave. During the argument which ensued, the older man suffered a heart attack. He and his wife blamed their daughter for this and evicted her from their home. The young woman then moved in with her boyfriend's family and has had no dealings with her own parents in years.

More ordinary tensions underlie most instances of separation between parents and children:

> In the Dodd household, teenaged Chuckie and his parents had engaged in petty disputes for years over such issues as the boy's curfew hour and driving habits. Since Mr. Dodd was a policeman, other officers chose to notify him whenever his son violated the traffic laws—which was rather often—instead of handling the youth formally. This made the father responsible to his colleagues for his son's behavior, so that the latter's misconduct was a great embarrassment to the older man. The final straw for Chuckie's parents came one evening when their son, now in his early 20s, left his van parked on the street illegally, took the keys, and went out with friends. When the police discovered the van, they called the young man's parents as usual. This time, however, the parents neither had the keys to move

the vehicle nor any idea of how to find their son, who had not told them where he was going. They therefore were forced to wait until he returned, knowing all the while that the husband's fellow officers were expecting the van to be moved. On this occasion, the youth did not come home until early sunrise. His parents then informed him that he would have to move out. The youth began to sleep at his place of employment and to shower at friends' homes. Shortly thereafter he found a place to live in another town.

It is generally a simpler and more common matter for a child to initiate a separation, since young people throughout the town routinely move out of their parents' homes with adulthood, even when everyone is on the best of terms. (If the child is underage, however, the parents may resist.) Simmering tensions between parent and child—which may have generated modified avoidance for years—are sometimes finally resolved only when a young person leaves home and cuts off all dealings with a mother or father.

Permanent avoidance represents an extreme of nonconfrontation in conflict management. The fact that it, more than any other sanction, lies in the background as the ultimate threat against offending family members does much to give moral order in Hampton its especially restrained and minimalistic quality. If conflicts cannot be dropped, if casual negotiation or mediation by intimates fails, if temporary or modified avoidance grows tiring, and if exhibiting emotional distress does not produce results, then Hamptonians will use disengagement.

Infrequent Responses

The complex of methods used by disputing relatives in Hampton differs from that found in many other settings partly in what it does not include or in what is uncommon. Confrontational tactics are comparatively infrequent, giving domestic order its tranquil character.

Violence, for example, although not unknown, is an unusual response to grievances in Hampton's families. People in the town can report few cases of actual or suspected domestic violence (other than that seen in the routine corporal punishment of small children or in the squabbles of such children among themselves), and they emphatically believe such behavior is rare. Official statistics concur in suggesting a low rate of family violence. Moreover, where aggression does occur, it tends to be comparatively mild. Hampton's citizens can recall only two domestic homicides. One involved a Southern woman who had just come to stay with family members when her estranged husband located her and killed her, and the other a woman who killed herself and her daughter during a conflict with her husband. Serious asssaults are likewise rare. Violence in Hampton is usually restricted to incidents such as one in which a man slapped his wife, or another in which a man whose son had defied him in getting a tattoo hit the tattoo with a spoon (causing bleeding which mixed the colors and ruined the design). Even these minor acts of violence are strongly condemned by the townspeople, however. Thus, unlike husbands and fathers in numerous societies (such as those of the Zinacanteco Indians of Mexico, the Qolla of the Andes, and the Jalé of New Guinea[19]), men in Hampton do not typically sanction their wives or older children with physical punishment; nor for their part are women and older children prone to aggression in their homes. Property destruction is also an infrequent sanction between relatives in Hampton. For most of the town's residents, domestic life is largely free of violence.

Violence of any kind may be understood as an effort to impose a unilateral settlement upon an opponent in a conflict. Since it plays such a small role in the domestic life of the town's residents, it is not surprising that authoritative rulings within the household are also comparatively unimportant in the management of disputes—at least those involving older children and adults. This too contrasts with the situation prevailing in the families of many other times and places. In ancient Greece and Rome, among traditional Irish peasants, in the homes of the Ashanti of Ghana, and in numerous other cases, senior male family members have wielded great power over those residing with them.[20] In these instances, they have been able for the most part to dictate the terms on which domestic disputes have been settled, imposing their will in disagreements involving themselves and adjudicating in the affairs of others. In Hampton, this authority is much weaker. Men sometimes claim it, but they are often met with resistance (or even laughter) when they do. Only over young children does their authority—and that of their wives—routinely prevail. In other cases, their position more closely approximates that of an influential *primus inter pares*—such as a "big man" among Melanesians,[21] whose word carries great weight but, in and of itself, is not always decisive. Like other family members, men usually resort to techniques beyond commands when they seek to handle their own conflicts or to intervene in the affairs of others.

Also insignificant in Hampton's moral order are informal tribunals, or moots, consisting of relatives assembled to deal collectively with conflicts involving two or more of their number. Gatherings of this sort—as described, for instance, among the Kpelle of Liberia, the Tiv of Nigeria, and the Ndendeuli of Tanzania[22]—have achieved great prominence in other settings, but they are virtually never found in Hampton. The much smaller households there rarely gather formally to debate and advise on any subject, including interpersonal tensions. Third-party intervention within families is restricted for the most part to spontaneous actions undertaken casually and informally.

Finally, intervention by nonfamily members is a comparatively infrequent occurrence during the course of domestic disputes. Few outsiders are asked by participants to help resolve conflict, and fewer still involve themselves on their own initiative. This is true of friends and neighbors as well as of formal agents of mediation and law. (Mental health professionals are in something of a special category in this regard, because their involvement generally entails no admission of conflict. Such people are defined as experts who help disturbed individuals overcome their personal difficulties, rather than as moral guardians or keepers of the peace. They are not asked to intervene in disputes, but only to help their patients recover. Because their relation to conflict is so indirect and so thoroughly denied, such professionals are usually more acceptable third parties than those whose role is more obvious. Even they, however, tend to become involved only in fairly exceptional cases of persistent conflict in which one of the parties exhibits signs of emotional distress.)

Residents of Hampton generally feel, as one official put it, that "people don't want their neighbors interfering in their affairs." What is more, it would appear that this perception is accurate. If neighbors overhear quarrels in progress, they almost always ignore them, and friends similarly are unlikely to become embroiled in a family's disputes. Only if asked to do so will they go so far as to give advice or support to one party, and then usually behind the scenes. (Thus, one woman routinely takes in her next-door neighbor for brief visits when the latter quarrels with her husband. Or, upon rare occasions in which violence occurs, a neighbor may call the police about a domestic quarrel in progress.) Generally, however, neighbors and friends neither volunteer nor are asked to play a role in family conflict. The situation seems similar to that in another suburb, where only 5 percent of a group of residents reported ever seeking the advice of friends or neighbors about a variety of routine domestic problems.[23]

Official third parties of various kinds are also unlikely to intervene on their own initiative. Only police, in response to a neighbor's call, will approach disputing family members who have not asked for their assistance. Others—ministers, lawyers, and judges—wait to be invoked by one or both parties. Thus, clergy members all report proceeding in the same way when someone tells them privately about a family's difficulties, or when they suspect them on their own. Taking advantage of their access to people's homes, they make a call upon that family or find some other means to encounter one of the parties casually. In this way they make themselves available should the family members be inclined to involve them in the resolution of their problem. If no one broaches the subject of the conflict, however, neither do they. One minister recounted as symbolic an episode in which he was visiting with a woman when her teenaged daughter burst out of a bedroom and began to scream at her. The woman calmly stood up, took the girl by the arm, led her back to the bedroom, and shut the door firmly. When she returned, she picked up the conversation where it had been left off. He considered it remarkable that the woman made no allusion at all to the scene he had witnessed; also noteworthy, however, is the fact that the minister himself did not pursue the matter. He had not been asked. Other third parties, notably lawyers and judges, are even more adamant about being approached by one of the parties themselves before intervening. Beyond this, all third parties, including legal officials, usually proceed in a more or less gingerly fashion when they know or suspect that one party resents their interference, regardless of how much the other might welcome it.

A great many of those uncommon situations in which people invoke formal third parties do not actually entail requests to come between disputing relatives and help work out a settlement. Instead, less intrusive services are often sought. Someone may ask a third party for private advice or moral support, for instance, as occurred when a woman whose husband was divorcing her to marry someone else turned to a minister for help in coping with this event. People may call upon third parties to defuse or terminate unusually hostile encounters, without asking them to meddle further in the causes or resolution of the conflict. This is a request made to the police (on average, about once every two or three days, often by the same families over and over) and to ministers (as when a woman summoned a clergyman to her home because she felt afraid of her husband). Finally, a large proportion of third-party involvement is incidental to the process of initiating permanent avoidance. This accounts for much recourse to lawyers and to family court, but also some to criminal law. For example, the police and municipal-court judge are sometimes called upon to deal with children who are "trespassing" after having been ordered from home. In fact, in many of the cases involving formal third parties, the antagonists are either on the verge of permanent separation (as is true of many couples who come for pastoral counseling) or are in the process of arranging it.

Regardless of the circumstances surrounding the invocation of a formal third party, it is generally the case that those the disputants approach are quite reluctant to take an active role. Ministers say that only "amateurs" would tell a disputing couple exactly how they think a problem should be solved. They rarely go further than to structure a dialogue through which people can work out their own solutions. Thus, the emphasis is upon self-help. Police officers too tend to shun forceful action when summoned to the scene of domestic disputes. A common approach which they take in such matters is to convince one party—usually the husband—to leave home for a few hours "until things calm down." They will virtually never make an arrest unless someone—again usually the husband—is abusive toward them. Nor do they engage in extensive substantive mediation in most cases.[24] And should a party pursue a matter to the criminal court—as 17 family members did in 40 court sessions held in Hampton during 1978 and 1979—the judge seldom will provide much intervention either. After listening to a brief description of the facts, he will usually put an offender on "informal probation"—suspending any sanction pending future good behavior—or counsel the parties to work out their own solution, and failing that, to separate.

This restriction of outside intervention in family conflict in Hampton differs from what is found in numerous other places. In many communities, outside involvement occurs frequently, whether the parties seek it or not.[25] In seventeenth-century colonial New Haven, to name one example, neighbors appear to have taken an active role in a family's disputes when these came to their attention. Thus, a case in the court records of the town describes how one Edward Camp and his wife "hearing a bustling, ran to see what was the matter" when Goodman and Goodwife Lines had a violent quarrel. They did not stop at breaking up the altercation, but went on to inquire into the circumstances of the affair and reproved Goodwife Lines for her conduct. Sometime later, Goodman Camp aired this matter in court as one of several grievances which *he* had against Goodwife Lines.[26] In this setting, magistrates and ministers also took an active interest in the townspeople's domestic affairs.[27] Similarly, in the rural Ireland of fifty years ago, parish priests seem to have intervened directly in the family troubles of their parishioners,[28] and an anthropologist who studied life among an African people, the Barotse, reports that legal officials there "constantly take the initiative to intervene in family disputes."[29] Furthermore, in these settings as in many others, intervention appears to have been unabashedly substantive and moralistic. Third parties seem to have spoken their minds freely and to have chided and scolded disputants they found to be in the wrong.[30] In Hampton, by contrast, third parties virtually never impose themselves, few are sought out to help manage a conflict, and, of those who do play a role, most are hesitant to intervene decisively. However a family dispute is managed, then, it is usually the family itself who sees to it. As a consequence, each family is largely a moral order unto itself.

· · ·

To summarize briefly at this point: Social control in Hampton's families consists for the most part of weak and restrained sanctions. Aside from inflicting minor deprivations, people who have disagreements with relatives generally restrict their response to dropping their conflicts, negotiating a settlement informally, submitting to the equally informal mediation of other family members, or temporarily avoiding an opponent. Should conflict persist and grow more serious, they may exhibit symptoms of personal distress, perhaps seeking psychiatric assistance, or opt for permanent avoidance. Only infrequently will they engage in violence, succeed in imposing a settlement of their own choosing, participate in a moot or family conclave, or invoke an outsider to weigh the merits of their cases and to suggest a resolution of their dispute.

Variations

Generally, people in Hampton deal with family grievances in similar ways. Nonetheless, there is an extent to which different sorts of people handle their domestic disagreements differently. The gender, age, and social class of the parties all appear to influence moral practice.

Gender

Faced with domestic conflict, women differ from men in at least one significant regard—they are more willing to invoke third parties. This is not to say that they turn to outsiders often, since, like men, they prefer to handle the great majority of problems on their own. Nonetheless, in those instances in which someone mobilizes a third party, it is more often a woman than a man who is responsible.

Thus, when neighbors or friends take a part in a family's disputes, it is usually a woman who turns to them. Similarly, women appear more likely than men to develop symptoms of emotional illness severe enough to prompt their recourse to a psychiatrist or other therapist. Like those subject to troublesome spirit possession in certain tribal societies,[31] and those who seek psychiatric therapy elsewhere in the contemporary United States,[32] those in Hampton who are most willing to invoke a therapist are female.

The same disparity exists in recourse to formal agents of mediation and social control. Women are more likely than men to initiate pastoral counseling, for example, and to seek a minister's assistance in convincing a recalcitrant husband to participate. One clergyman reports that when men do approach him for advice, they are more likely than women to do so casually, bringing up their problem in a seemingly spontaneous way during the course of ordinary conversation. They are less willing than women to make an appointment and to admit openly that they would like a minister's participation in their affairs.

Legal officials too receive disproportionately many requests for assistance from women. When the police are summoned to the scene of a domestic dispute, it is virtually always a woman who calls them. This, too, accords with patterns in other American settings.[33] At the local municipal court, all but one of 17 complaints involving family members heard during 40 sessions in 1978 and 1979 were initiated by women—wives against husbands, mothers against sons, and sisters against brothers.[34]

The greater willingness of women to involve outside third parties in domestic affairs sometimes means that men are faced with the intrusion of people whose presence they resent. Their frequently strong opposition is one factor in the hesitance of many third parties to take an active role in cases of domestic conflict. It also underlies most arrests which occur when police intervene in domestic altercations. In one illustrative case, two police officers arrested a man who insulted them with ethnic slurs, shoved one of them, and ordered them from his home when they answered a call from his wife. The same resistance sometimes surfaces in court. One young man pointedly explained to the judge that he was pleading guilty to an assault charge lodged by his sister so that he would not "have to go into a lot of family business that is not the court's concern." He steadfastly refused to describe the circumstances leading to his argument with his sister, saying that "it would take too long" to do so.

It is possible that if male resistance to outside third parties were less extreme than it is, more women might call upon them. In other words, some women may forego mobilizing outsiders because they know how negatively their husbands would respond. In general, however, it is important to reemphasize that recourse to third parties does not seem an attractive option to either sex. Most women, like most men, keep their family problems in the home.

Age

Two features of social control within families are affected most noticeably by the age of the participants. One is the degree of coercion and violence involved in conflict situations; the other is the frequency of recourse to outside third parties. In regard to the former, it might be observed that coercion is a prominent element of domestic control only when the offender is a young child. Parents routinely inflict minor physical sanctions on small boys and girls, although not severe ones, and children make greater use than adults do of petty violence among themselves. The actual conduct rarely exceeds spanking, where adults are participants, or punching and kicking, where the parties are all children. More serious violence is not only uncommon, but thoroughly disapproved of by wider public sentiment.

Authoritative commands are also more common and more successful when a parent has a grievance against a small child. As children grow older and reach adolescence, however, they begin to resist such commands with increasing vigor and effectiveness. Their rebelliousness often comes as an initially unpleasant surprise to their parents, who have been accustomed to greater deference. During the period in which children give up the role of small child and assume that of adult, their disputes with their parents often escalate in frequency, vehemence, and duration. One adult, after describing a series of conflicts between a teenaged boy and his parents over such issues as the boy's hair style, clothes, curfew, and guitar practices, remarked, "That tells the story of half of Hampton."

The other difference apparent in strategies of conflict management across age groups pertains to the use of third parties. Like women in comparison to men, young people are more willing than adults to bring their family disputes before the attention of outsiders. This is specifically the case where friends are concerned. Young people are more likely than older ones to air their domestic problems before peers and to solicit their advice. They also turn to them more often for some kinds of assistance, such as help in circumventing parental efforts at deprivation. The willingness of young people to tell their friends details of their domestic disputes often vexes adults, who are more inclined to keep such information to themselves. In fact, older people tend in general to view young people as indiscreet. (It is an interesting sidelight on this attribution that a juvenile officer once remarked how much he prefers to deal with youthful suspects in the absence of their parents. "The kids," he said, "like to tell you what they've done. They're proud of it. It's the adults who won't let them talk.")

Young people are also more prone to exhibit severe symptoms of emotional distress and personal maladjustment. Although, unlike adult women, they rarely have the personal financial resources to contact a therapist on their own intiative, their conduct sometimes leads a parent to suggest this or leads to the intervention of teachers, guidance counselors, or the police. And even when no formal third party becomes involved, signs of distress often attract notice from outsiders and publicize a young person's grievance. On the other hand, open recourse to formal agents of mediation and social control is less common among the young, perhaps partly because their grievances elicit less concern from such people. Thus, when a ten-year-old girl appeared at the police station one day to sign a complaint against her mother, who had hit her and locked her out of the house, she was told that the law does not allow children to proceed in this way against their parents.

Social Class

There are several ways in which patterns of conflict management in working-class families differ from those in middle-class ones, although the two classes both share a preference for restraint in the face of grievances and are more similar than different in their moral practices. As a group, working-class families are more likely than others to confront and handle conflicts directly, rather than ignore and contain them. Thus, for instance, the greater proximity of extended family members within the working-class community means that there are more third parties available to intervene when conflicts arise. Older parents, grown siblings, in-laws, and other relatives may step between disputing parties to engage in friendly peacemaking, to mediate a settlement, or simply to give their advice. One husband turned to his sister for help when he found his wife's behavior erratic and deteriorating, for example, and a wife called upon her mother-in-law for assistance when her husband became interested in another woman.

Related to the greater availability of third parties who can help focus and resolve conflict is a correspondingly less extensive use of avoidance in working-class homes. Virtually all of the more extreme cases of temporary avoidance uncovered—those in which people refused to speak at all for weeks or months at a time—involved middle-class people. There is also a difference in the incidence of divorce in the two classes. Although national statistics for the United States as a whole show that divorces decline as income and status rise,[35] under the conditions prevailing in Hampton it is the higher-income middle class that resorts to divorce more often. Since research in other settings has shown that the presence of an interconnected network of social contacts surrounding married couples undermines divorce,[36] the greater proximity of extended family members to working-class people in Hampton seems an important factor in their lower rate of marital dissolution.

Some features of the working-class situation involve more force, rather than more settlement, in the face of grievances. One pattern pertains to the degree and kind of social control found among teenaged siblings. In working-class families, brothers and sisters engage in more frequent and more intense regulation of one another's conduct. The sheer range of behavior with which they concern themselves is wider, and their responses to perceived infractions stronger. They are more likely than middle-class siblings to feel that the actions of one reflect on them all. In fact, although there is no conclusive evidence that either class exceeds the other in the general exercise of domestic violence, and although townspeople themselves either claim no difference or offer contradictory opinions on the matter, it appears that working-class siblings are more physically aggressive toward one another than middle-class siblings are.

A notable case in point is the social control of sexuality. While middle-class siblings are generally tolerant or indifferent about one another's sex lives, working-class siblings are less so. In particular, working-class brothers are likely to be concerned about their sisters' romantic involvements, and frequently take direct action to discourage or curtail them. In one case, a youth became very upset when his thirteen-year-old sister began dating a man in his early twenties. He ordered the sister to break off the relationship, but she refused to do so. When it became apparent that the couple would indeed continue to see each other, the youth took matters into his own hands and beat both the girl and her boyfriend. He felt that the beating was necessary to prevent his sister from becoming a notoriously promiscuous woman like their mother. In a similar case, one evening a teenaged youth overheard some acquaintances telling others that his sister was available for sex in a local graveyard. The youth stormed to the scene immediately, where he found a group of boys with his sister. (The incident had begun with the girl a willing participant, but by the time her brother arrived the whole affair had gotten out of her control.) The youth broke up the gathering by ordering the males to leave, which they did. He then beat his sister severely for her promiscuity. A third conflict between siblings arose when a youth learned from schoolmates that his sister had had a second abortion. He confronted the girl in a high-school corridor and, although others were present, began to berate her loudly. Among other things, he told her that she was a "disgrace to the family." The girl responded by hitting her brother, and the two scuffled briefly until friends pulled them apart. It is worth observing in this context that along with the greater forcefulness of social control exerted by working-class siblings against each other, there also exists a greater willingness to undertake social control against others on a sibling's behalf. In one case, for example, a teenaged girl's family became very concerned that her boyfriend was hitting her. The girl herself never told them so, but they were able to deduce this from her injuries. When the situation persisted, one of the girl's brothers approached her boyfriend and threatened violence if he ever struck the girl again.

Another way in which working-class families engage in more confrontation can be seen in the circumstances surrounding permanent avoidance between parents and children. In middle-class families, it is customary for young people to go away to college when they are about eighteen years old. It is also common for children to take employment beyond the immediate geographic area. As a result, many parents and children in a state of conflict with one another are separated by what is considered the natural course of the life-cycle. Permanent avoidance is easily begun, with the young people slipping away quietly. In working-class families, however, there is no equally clear-cut point at which teenagers are expected to leave their parents' home. Only a general idea that young people will move away some time after high-school graduation prevails. Therefore, in working-class families tensions between parents and teenagers are not so readily interrupted, and they more frequently escalate to the point at which the adults angrily demand that a young person leave home. Evictions of this sort more often involve working-class people.

Finally, one other difference between the classes is noteworthy, and that pertains to the use of third parties in conflict situations. Although middle-class people involve therapists more often—a pattern consistent with what occurs elsewhere in the United States,[37] and one which has been attributed to their greater individuation and the looseness of their social ties[38]—and although the divorces more often obtained by middle-class people virtually coerce the use of lawyers and family-court judges, it is working-class people who more often seek out a direct and detailed involvement of criminal law in their domestic disputes. Thus, the police are more likely to participate in working-class family conflicts. The greater willingness of working-class people to invoke them is nicely illustrated by the response of two men from different classes to essentially identical conduct by their daughters. In the first case, a man from a working-class family who had recently opened a small delicatessen had a quarrel with his teenaged daughter about her sex life. As a result, the girl left home and took up residence in the house of a friend. Although the people who offered her shelter seemed willing to keep her with them indefinitely, at their own expense, the girl's father objected to this arrangement and demanded that his daughter return home. After a short while, he called the police to ask that they pick up the girl and bring her back. There followed a few days during which the young woman, with the help of friends, eluded the police, but eventually she was found and returned to her family. The second case is that of Sheila McCarthy (see pp. 25-26). She also ran away from home and was willingly taken in by a friend's family, a situation that proved unacceptable to her abandoned father. What is pertinent about this case is that her middle-class father never asked the police to intervene, although Sheila lived openly in her friend's home for weeks. He simply did not want police involvement and chose to pursue the issue in other ways.

So strong is the middle-class aversion to calling the police against intimates that many people who decide to seek emergency outside intervention—a rare occurrence in any case—prefer to call ministers instead. From the accounts of Hampton's clergy, it appears that Protestant ministers are more likely than Catholic priests (whose congregation includes a large proportion of working-class people) to be summoned to homes at mealtime and during the evening to interrupt domestic disputes. People also occasionally call a minister about a neighboring family's altercation, again bypassing the police. Members of the clergy feel that they are summoned in large part because their presence at a home attracts little attention from outsiders. They reportedly respond to emergency calls promptly as long as they know at least one of the disputing parties.

Far from bringing the police into their personal relationships, the middle-class residents of Hampton evidence little respect for them. One elderly middle-class woman remarked that the police are "just public *servants*" (her emphasis) who sometimes "forget their place." What the police have to say about their affairs means comparatively little to middle-class people. When an officer accuses their children of misconduct, for instance, middle-class parents are less likely to accept the accusation than are working-class parents. The officer in charge of juvenile matters prefers to deal with what he calls "blue-collar families" for just this reason, remarking that "If I call a blue-collar parent about a kid, the parent will say, 'He did *what*? I'll bring him right down.' If I call a white-collar parent, the parent will say, 'What did he allegedly do? I'll be right down with my lawyer.'"

This differing degree of deference toward the police is illustrated by an incident in which teenagers from both classes attended a party at an abandoned house in a wooded setting in town. Alerted by the nearest neighbor that someone was in the house, the police arrived to find the young people drinking alcoholic beverages and listening to music. The officers called for reinforcements and proceeded to take into custody all those young people under the legal drinking age, whether they had actually been seen with liquor or not. Some of the teenagers managed to escape into the woods, but many were brought to the police station. The officer in charge then called all the parents of those picked up and asked them to come to the station for their children. As the parents arrived, a significant difference in their attitudes toward the event was evident, the working-class parents generally treating the matter as considerably more serious. Many showed anger; one addressed the group of teenagers, saying earnestly that his home was always available to them if they wanted to party and exhorting them not to get into the same trouble again. The middle-class parents, by contrast, tended to relate to the scene more casually. Once the young people were home, the working-class parents were more likely to sanction them. One girl was deprived of Easter dinner the next day and could have only bread and water at a family gathering. Her parents announced that if she wanted to act like a criminal, she would have to get used to being treated like one. In several middle-class homes, on the other hand, the incident was dismissed as humorous.

A similar difference in the reactions of middle-class and working-class people appears in the treatment of two juvenile shoplifters by their parents. The family of a working-class boy who had stolen a hat branded him a "thief" and treated him so coldly that one of the juvenile authorities called the boy's mother on his behalf. In the second case, the mother of a middle-class girl who had likewise shoplifted an item of small value defended her daughter. The woman at first denied that the girl could possibly have taken anything, and then, confronted by the testimony of the merchant who had seen the incident, found a way to excuse the matter. Her daughter, she said, had not eaten any breakfast on the morning in question and her judgment must have been impaired by hypoglycemia.

The greater willingness of working-class people to use law against family members can also be seen strikingly in the municipal court. In Hampton, cases involving people in ongoing relationships are almost always brought before the municipal judge on the basis of a complaint which one private citizen signs against another, and all such complaints receive a hearing. The complainants themselves prosecute the cases in court, sometimes assisted by a private attorney but in the great majority of instances on their own. In either case, the process constitutes private prosecution of crime, a phenomenon rarely seen in the courts of more urban American settings. During 40 court sessions in 1978 and 1979, there were 17 cases involving complaints between family members. All but 2 of these—or about 88 percent—involved working-class people.

In addition, only two cases in which people complained to an administrative officer or an elected official during the course of domestic conflict were uncovered, and both of these involved working-class individuals. In one case, a working-class man approached the sanitarians at the Board of Health to complain that his grown son and the latter's family refused to move out and to set up a separate residence of their own. The man wondered if there might not be a law prohibiting "too many" people from living in one house. To his disappointment, he was told that since he owned his own home there was no law covering the situation. In the other instance, a working-class family called the mayor during the course of a dispute with in-laws over the ownership of a piece of property.

Thus, overall, working-class people experience a greater amount of open and substantive third-party intervention in their domestic conflicts than middle-class people. Middle-class people, when they involve outsiders at all, are more likely to turn to therapists for "problems" not defined as conflicts, or to individuals who are needed simply to facilitate permanent avoidance. In fact, all of the differences between the classes in domestic conflict management—modest as these are—show working-class people more prone to exercise direct and forceful responses to family tensions. Nonetheless, it bears repeating that all people in Hampton tend for the most part to proceed against offending relatives in similar ways, and these are ways most notable for restraint and the containment of hostilities.

Toward a Theory of Moral Minimalism

Several factors appear to contribute to the spare and restrained character of domestic social control in Hampton. In other words, the moral minimalism that prevails in the town's families seems a composite creation of various social forces, some of which encourage moral calm directly and others of which discourage open confrontation. These factors are internal—having to do with the organization of family life itself—and external—pertaining to the situation of families in the larger community. The internal factors especially foster avoidance, while the external ones undermine recourse to third parties and their substantive intervention. Presumably, wherever comparable factors exist in any setting, moral minimalism will be encouraged. Before considering these matters in more detail, however, it is important to confront one explanation of moral minimalism—whether in families, neighborhoods, or any other setting—that might initially seem credible. This is the notion that moral minimalism somehow results from the nature of the offenses to which it responds.

The Seriousness of Offenses

To some it might appear that moral restraint naturally arises where offensive behavior is trivial, that weak responses express minor grievances, and that if transgressions were more serious, more forceful reactions would be found. It might be thought, for example, that people react more violently when faced with more serious problems and that this explains aggression. A similar argument might be advanced to explain a greater propensity to use law, mediation, or other confrontational techniques for resolving conflict.[39] But there are difficulties with such claims.

The seriousness of an offense is defined in practice by the response to it.[40] Where moral minimalism prevails, offenses are apt to appear trivial to an observer precisely because their victims react with such restraint. There have been and still are many social settings in which the sorts of misconduct found in suburbia would be treated as serious and would elicit strong countermeasures, including violence. In some cases, they might initiate a process of escalating conflict that culminated in the use of extreme force. In others, they might lead to exhaustive efforts at settlement.

The human capacity to react strongly to offenses of any nature was satirized several centuries ago by Jonathan Swift in his fictional work, *Gulliver's Travels*. There, he described a dreadful conflict in a distant land that erupted over the issue of the proper way to break an egg—whether at the small end or large. As a result of this question, "there have been six rebellions raised"; "it is computed that eleven thousand persons have, at several times, suffered death, rather than submit to break their eggs at the smaller end"; and "a bloody war hath been carried on between . . . two empires for six and thirty moons."[41] Real life affords numerous other examples that serve to make the same point. In medieval France, a war broke out when one lord remarked that another looked like a blacksmith.[42] Duels—and duelling fatalities—were once common in Europe over such everyday issues as insults, slights, and competition for the favors of women. In one recorded instance, a fatal duel arose over a dogfight:

> The two men involved were riding that morning in Hyde Park, each followed by a Newfoundland dog, when the dogs started fighting. [One man] separated the animals, exclaiming, "Whose dog is that? I will knock him down!" [The other man] replied, "Have you the

impudence to say that you will knock my dog down? You must first knock me down!" High words ensued, followed by an exchange of cards and an agreement to meet at seven o'clock that evening.[43]

In contemporary America, most assaults and homicides occur in the course of disputes originating from an array of everyday annoyances that suburbanites usually tolerate or handle with avoidance. This is true within families as well as outside them. One study has found that precipitating factors in typical cases of domestic violence are nothing more dramatic than disagreements over children, money, sex, housekeeping, or social activities.[44] Insults also appear capable of provoking much aggression. In an illustrative case from New York City, an unmarried couple living together

> were both drinking and apparently they both started to insult each other. It wasn't clear who struck first, but the common-law husband struck his wife with a shovel, hitting her in the eye, and she struck him in the arm with an exacto knife, causing injury.[45]

In an account of his life in an urban slum, a man described how he confronted his father with a gun for calling his mother a "bitch."[46] Outside the family, insults and minor annoyances can also generate considerable violence. One investigator tells of a man who killed another at an automobile raceway during an argument over a spilt beer.[47] Another recounts an episode in which the police were called to intervene in an explosive situation arising when a customer in a luncheonette contested a 10-cent charge for lettuce and tomato on his sandwich.[48] In New York City, a woman threw a bucket of lye in a neighbor's face because the latter had struck her daughter.[49] In a case presented as typical of those handled by urban mediation programs, one man broke another's arm in a scuffle arising from a disagreement over a blocked driveway.[50] More generally, in a survey of all the homicides occurring in Philadelphia over a four-year period, a sociologist concluded that a third of the deaths—the modal category—resulted from "altercations of relatively trivial origin; insult, curse, jostling, etc." Another 14 percent took place during domestic quarrels.[51] The investigator made the following observations:

Intensive reading of the police files and of verbatim reports of interrogations, as well as participant observation in these interrogations by the author suggest that the significance of a jostle, a slightly derogatory remark, or the appearance of a weapon in the hands of an adversary are stimuli differentially perceived and interpreted by Negroes and whites, males and females. Social expectations of response in particular types of social interaction result in differential "definitions of the situation" . . . . The upper middle and upper class value system . . . considers many of the social and personal stimuli that evoke a combative reaction in the lower classes as "trivial."[52]

A later survey of homicide in Houston confirms the Philadelphia findings, recounting cases in which people were killed during arguments arising over such matters as a wife's disapproval of a $40 loan taken out by her husband, the right of a stepparent to discipline a child, the claim of two drivers to the same parking space, and even a young man's demand for a share of his friend's french fries.[53]

If the seriousness of grievances cannot account for violence, neither can it account for recourse to law. There are many societies around the world which have no formal legal system at all, even for coping with offenses viewed as very serious by their victims. On the other hand, in our society and elsewhere, people often resort to law over matters that might strike observers as trivial. In colonial New Haven, for example, one of the most frequent charges brought before the court was that someone had defamed another, usually by a simple insult of some kind.[54] Thus, when Bamfield Bell, angered by William Paine's reproof of his "profane" singing, retaliated by accusing Paine of being "one of the holy brethren who will lye for advantage," Paine took legal action against him.[55] Similarly, among the Lipay of the Philippines, where litigation is reported to be exceptionally frequent and a source of entertainment for the population, "a large share, if not the majority, of legal cases deal with offenses so minor that only the fertile imagination of a [native] legal authority can magnify them into a serious threat to some person or to society in general."[56] Here as in colonial New Haven, "slandering, malicious gossip, false accusations, [and] insults" are common allegations.[57]

The same pattern can be seen in the Soviet Union, where citizens can appeal to Comrades' Courts to handle a wide variety of grievances encountered in everyday life. Illustrative cases reported in the Soviet press involve people who have complained of others for "squabbling and defaming and insulting" their fellow workers, for showing "an exceptionally coarse and cynical attitude toward their neighbors," and for missing work because of drunkenness.[58] Other cases arise over the frustrations of crowded apartments, such as one in which "it is reported that B asked the Comrades' Court of a housing office to require her neighbor, S, to make room in their communal kitchen for B's chair. S already had three of her own chairs in the apparently small kitchen."[59] Examples such as these from numerous other societies and settings abound.

The seriousness of offenses is also an inadequate explanation for the invocation of moots and other forms of mediation in societies where these are available to aggrieved parties. Again, many of the issues aired in this way would simply be tolerated or processed with restraint in a setting where moral minimalism prevailed. Examples from the Ndendeuli of Tanzania, whose moots have been particularly well described, help to make the point. There, one moot was convened by a man whose principal complaint was that his cousin had slighted him by not inviting him to a beer party. He also alleged that members of the cousin's family had insulted his wife and broken one of her water pots, and had amused themselves at his expense "by likening him to a strutting cock" and caricaturing his walk and gestures.[60] Another moot amounted principally to "a general complaint by a father-in-law against his son-in-law's behavior"; the triggering incident occurred when the son-in-law failed to heed his father-in-law's request for help in hauling and putting into place two new wall posts for his house.[61]

In light of this, it should be obvious that moral minimalism, wherever it occurs, cannot be ascribed to the inherent triviality of offenses. The transgressions and annoyances found in suburban families, for example, are not necessarily conducive to the restrained responses that they encounter there. Under appropriate social conditions, the homes of these peaceful people could as well be the sites of numerous assaults and murders; the parks could be the scenes of pitched battles or moots; the courtroom could be bulging with cases. The conclusion is inescapable that it is not the substance of grievances but rather the organization of social life which explains the distinctively peaceful moral order of suburbia, including that of its families.

The Theory of Avoidance

Ultimately, it is the internal organization of family life in Hampton that seems most responsible for the weak and restrained character of what usually happens when relatives dispute. Family members from both classes take comparatively little forceful or positive action against one another, it would appear, so often choosing merely to avoid instead, largely because their domestic relations are so loose-knit by the standards of people in other times and places. Another way of stating this is to say that suburban families are comparatively weak families, and that this characteristic in turn breeds a relative absence of social control.

Along many dimensions by which strength and intensity of domestic life might be assessed, families in Hampton appear strikingly low in these traits. They are, for one thing, quite small, since with few exceptions households contain no more than one adult man, one adult woman, and their children. Only a minority of the population—mostly from the town's working class—have any extended family members living in other households in the town. On a day-by-day basis, people in these small families follow dispersed and individuated routines. Very few collective activities bring the group together to work side by side for a common purpose, in the way that agriculture and crafts structure the interaction of relatives in some more traditional settings. If the capacity for collective action and the frequency of its execution are taken to define organization,[62] then Hampton's families are rather unorganized. The bulk of those joint ventures that they do undertake are restricted to the discretionary realm of pleasure and leisure, and do not play a crucial role in the pursuit of material necessities.

Instead of working together on a frequent basis for the good of the group, most family members in Hampton actually spend a great deal of time on their own or with nonrelatives. Virtually all adult men, and many adult women, have jobs that require them to be absent from their families—and Hampton altogether—for at least one-fourth of the hours in a week. All but the youngest children similarly go off to school regularly. Beyond the commitment of time to jobs and classes, other pursuits—doing things with friends, studying at the library, jogging or weightlifting at the local YMCA, attending club meetings or political gatherings, to name just a few—also separate family members from one another.

Even within the home, dispersion is usual. Most houses in Hampton are large enough to permit spatial separation, and the town's residents exploit this. (In Hampton an average of 3 persons per household share an average of 7 rooms per residence; while space in the average working-class home appears somewhat tighter than in the average middle-class home, there are many individual exceptions and the average differences are not great.) Private bedrooms for each child are the ideal, for instance, and people will move to new homes or build additions to their present ones in order to arrange it. Much time in the home is spent in these enclaves, away from other relatives. Beyond this, it is common for there to be so many communal rooms that people tend to spread themselves out among them. A kitchen, dining room, living room, den or recreation room, one or more porches, and two or more bathrooms, are all typical.

Corresponding to physical separation, and intensifying its effects, is the fact that family members in Hampton strive to minimize joint ownership of possessions.[63] Indeed, the division of a house into numerous private spaces can be interpreted partly as a way to circumvent shared use of the dwelling. As far as a family's means allow—and in an affluent suburb this is quite far—people avoid having to share possessions and tend to accumulate an extensive amount of private property. Just a few of the objects frequently acquired for each member of a household who uses them are radios, stereos, television sets, clothes, telephone numbers, toiletries, cars, and a variety of incidentals. People rightly perceive that joint use of objects can generate conflicts—many disputes in families do in fact arise when people who must share something disagree about its disposition—and their inclination when faced with difficulties of this kind is to get enough of the objects in question to satisfy everyone, as soon as possible. By this means, resources are made plentiful rather than scarce; since scarcity is known to breed conflict,[64] such tactics preserve the peace. The entire process is assisted by the fact that, at least from their early teenaged years, young people have access to small sums of money obtained independently of their parents.

Another way in which Hampton's families are comparatively weak is in their long-term hold on their members. To an extent unusual among kin groups throughout history and across the world, they are voluntary associations whose members are not bound to one another through time by material necessity. Escape to a comfortable life completely without relatives is possible for everyone, either immediately or in due course, so that family members do not control one another's destinies in Hampton. The situation is far different from that which prevails even elsewhere in modern societies, in communities of the very poor where family members need one another's financial contribution desperately and make strong efforts to maintain connections.[65] The normal run of the affluent suburban life-cycle will ultimately disperse families around the country, away from one another except for occasional sociable interaction on visits or by telephone.

The weakness of domestic life in Hampton, as seen in all of the features just discussed, undermines forceful or direct responses to grievances in several ways. (It also prevents some grievances from arising at all.) Perhaps most important, it makes avoidance—both temporary and permanent—a feasible and attractive option to relatives in conflict. The availability and ease of avoidance in any setting seem to depend on a complex of conditions, including not only physical avenues of escape but also social ones created by such factors as the *fluidity* of social relationships, with individuals meeting and parting frequently on a routine basis; the *dispersion* of people, with individuals scattered across a variety of pursuits and locations and interacting with each other only part of the time; the *atomization* of people, with each person acting as an individual rather than as part of a larger corporate group whose interests are at stake in all social dealings; and *material independence* among people, with subsistence possible for all even in the face of separation and with few possessions held in common.[66]

It has been hypothesized that where social conditions make the costs of avoidance low, so that people are able to leave conflict-ridden relationships without jeopardizing their own interests, separation in the face of conflict will be routine.[67] In fact, earlier studies have indicated that those who are able simply to disengage from hostilities will generally do so rather than escalate a dispute; in other words, avoidance seems to be a recourse of first resort. Thus, ease of separation accounts for the fact that so many people in the simplest societies—those of the nomadic and socially fluid hunters and gatherers—depend on avoidance to resolve conflict, while fewer people in the more interdependent and sedentary communities of agriculturalists do so.[68] Those exceptional farming societies in which there is a great deal of avoidance tend to be ones in which an abundance of land and water, along with the nature of agricultural technique, promote easy and routine movements of people. An example can be found in the Majangir of Ethiopia, whose pattern of shifting cultivation requires frequent changes of residence and who are characterized by "small clusters of dispersed homesteads and dispersed huts within homesteads, . . . impermanent habitations . . . , [and a lack] of livestock and fixed property."[69] In the face of conflict, Majangir individuals routinely separate.[70]

The same principle explains other cases of avoidance. On the wagon trains that bore nineteenth-century Americans westward, those who wanted to could readily divide any joint property and continue on their way independently; many did so in response to disagreements, even going so far as to saw four-wheeled wagons in half so that each of two disputants could maintain the use of a vehicle.[71] Similarly, British colonial administrators who could not get along with their fellows in one location could always request a transfer elsewhere, and this was a principal way in which such people handled their conflicts.[72] Another instance can be seen in the situation of at least some contemporary American nuns who, like the colonial administrators, have the ability to request new assignments to other places if something about their living situation displeases them. Under these circumstances, conflict between sisters is often resolved when one party simply moves away.[73] The ease of severing an unsatisfying relationship also explains why, in contemporary market economies where many firms supply the same products and where people are free to shop where they choose, disgruntled customers generally respond by simply taking their business elsewhere.[74]

The absence of possibilities for avoidance, on the other hand, encourages the use of alternative tactics of conflict management. In one specific case, the traditionally peaceful Chenchu of the Indian subcontinent became quite violent when they were detained on reservations without the ability to separate in the face of disputes as they had previously done.[75] And the emergence of the earliest states historically has been explained by factors that limited the possibilities for avoidance, such as the expansion of populations up to geographic limits imposed by barriers such as oceans, rivers, and mountain ranges. Across these barriers, avoidance was not possible, so that people who had previously separated in the face of interpersonal tension had to develop new ways of coping with ever-increasing conflict.[76]

Consistent with all of this, family members in Hampton often contain their conflicts by taking advantage of numerous opportunities to restrict contact with one another, both outside the home and even inside it. Separate activities, separate rooms, separate possessions, and the capacity for separate livelihoods mean that people do not have to interact. If tensions persist over time, relatives can move apart and start a new life. Indeed, the sheer possibility of future escape, and frequently the expectation of eventual separation, seem by themselves to discourage the use of aggressive sanctions. This too is true outside of the suburbs. It has been reported that among the Qolla of the Andes, for example, physical punishment of wives by husbands increases substantially following a formal ceremony which takes place some time after spouses begin living together, since then divorce becomes much more difficult.[77] In Hampton, the lesser tendency of middle-class siblings—who are unlikely to live near one another in adulthood—to evaluate one another's conduct and to impose sanctions is consistent with the notion that anticipated separation in itself undermines confrontation. Along similar lines, the fact that Hampton's middle-class parents evict older children less often than working-class parents do becomes understandable in light of the routine separation of parents and children found in the middle class.

The possibility of avoidance, and indeed the dispersion of family members on a day-to-day basis, allows tensions to cool and arguments to "blow over" while people are apart. The same conditions also lessen any inherent pressures for settlement that might generate extensive efforts at negotiation and mediation or frequent recourse to outside third parties. Since relatives need not and do not operate collectively except for pleasure, the welfare of the group is not compromised by ill will between two of its members and little of importance need go undone because people are avoiding one another. In their autonomy, other relatives may hardly be affected by a dispute within their household, and the principals themselves may experience few alterations in their affairs.

The weak hold which families have on their members not only fosters avoidance directly but also undermines internal authority. People who are not able to supervise and to monitor one another's conduct are in a poor position to enforce their wills. Many attempts by adults to dictate what their older children ought to do founder on exactly this point; the young people simply go off by themselves or with their friends and do just as they wish anyway. Far more important is the fact that relatives in Hampton have so little control over one another's futures. Where patriarchal families are the norm, or families in which a handful of elders have great power, it seems generally the case that individuals there are dependent on kin groups to secure their futures. Sometimes this dependency never ends, and people always need their relatives to give them a respectable place in the community. In other cases, the dependency exists until a turning point at which time a person's situation becomes established once and for all, as occurs when a young person inherits land or resources without which he or she could lead only an impoverished or stigmatized life. In Hampton, however, families do not have such importance. Husbands cannot hold the specter of chronic penury, isolation, scorn, or other hardship before their wives and children, nor can the reverse occur. Substantial independence is the result, rendering family members free to defy or ignore one another's commands. Further-

more, all of this is intensified by the fact that even on an immediate basis all but young children have (at least potentially) access
to some material resources outside the family.[78] In this light, the
greater susceptibility of young children to physical punishment
and parental authority seems to arise both from their more restricted resources in the short term and from the longer time they
must spend in the family before they can exploit the alternatives
ultimately available to them. It is significant, however, that even
when their children are very young many parents in Hampton
begin trying to "establish a good relationship" with them. At some
level they are aware that unless they can bind their children to
them with ties of affection, no material compulsion will keep those
children deferential to them—or even in touch with them—in
later years.

The Theory of the Third Party

A significant component of the weak, restrained, and minimalistic
quality of social control in Hampton's families is the fact that
people there handle most domestic disputes on their own. If
outsiders volunteered their intervention as frequently as they do in
certain other places, or if principals in conflict sought third-party
assistance more often, disputants would be more frequently com-
pelled to confront their problems directly and to come to terms
with them. Furthermore, since third parties are often capable of
exercising at least some sanctions of their own to enforce a settlement, their intervention would entail a degree of coercion otherwise absent from the process of conflict management. Part of the
explanation for Hampton's minimalistic style of domestic social
control thus lies in the minor role played by outside third parties in
disputes.

The social distance that separates households from one
another in the town helps to explain why third-party intervention
is so uncommon. Each family in Hampton is a distinct and autonomous entity, carefully demarcated from others physically and
relationally. Thus, most people live in single-family detached
houses, protected by expanses of lawn and walls of shrubs from
too-close proximity to others. No shared property (beyond a few

municipal parks rarely used by anyone) or material dependence, few communal activities, and little enforced association bind even the nearest neighbors or any but the most exceptional of friends. Separate associates, separate jobs, and separate interests serve as centrifugal forces in the social networks that exist. Beyond this, since relatively frequent residential mobility is a prominent feature of middle-class life in Hampton, many people tend to have short pasts and short futures in common with their fellows in the town. This restricts the amount of knowledge individuals have about one another and introduces another measure of distance. It has been suggested that intimacy between people may be measured by the "scope, frequency, and length" of their interaction, "the age of their relationship, and the nature and number of links between them in a social network."[79] On all of these counts, the ties between unrelated people in Hampton tend to be weak.

It seems clear that the involvement of third parties in the conflicts of others increases as their intimacy with the principals intensifies. People are both more apt to intervene in the affairs of those to whom they are close and to be asked to intervene by them. In societies and settings where third-party participation is high, it is generally the case that people know one another well and are closely tied to each other. It is understandable then that third parties are of such little prominence in the conflicts of Hampton's relatives, except when they are themselves close family members.

The significance of intimacy may explain some of the differences among people in their use of third parties. Thus, those women who are not employed outside the home and who spend more time in their neighborhoods accordingly forge somewhat stronger ties to one another and are also more likely to seek neighborly assistance when domestic troubles arise. Similarly, young people have unusually strong and intimate friendships by adult standards, and more often turn to their friends for support and advice during disputes with their parents and siblings. Working-class people, having more close relatives nearby, experience more third-party participation in their affairs. And even though most people are equally distant from formal third parties of various kinds, it is sometimes possible to see the influence of intimacy in their use as well. Ministers, for instance, report receiving more requests for advice and assistance the longer they have been in the community, and more from religious people at all times.

In addition to social atomization and autonomy, the high status of Hampton's families may also discourage people from turning to outsiders for help with their personal difficulties. This would be understandable in light of more general patterns of dispute settlement. Submitting a conflict to third-party intervention (especially in its more coercive forms such as arbitration and adjudication) entails a compromise of autonomy and a kind of subordination of the disputants to the outside party or parties involved.[80] For this reason, high-status people often limit third-party involvement except under certain conditions. Should their opponents be of lower status, for instance, their reluctance may be overcome by the tendency of outsiders simply to side with the higher-status parties and give them victory.[81] Under these circumstances, officials may function simply to support rather than to evaluate high-status disputants. People of high status may also consent to outside intervention if an issue in dispute touches on their economic interests. But where private relationships with relatives and other status peers are involved, the subordination entailed may be repugnant unless even higher-status people are available to intervene.

In fact, where social stratification exists, there is generally an upward drift of disputes in which higher-status people are called upon to settle the affairs of those beneath them. Thus, for instance, it has been noted that in an Indian village

> the dominant caste plays a very important role in the settlement of disputes . . . . The leaders of the dominant caste not only settle disputes between members of different castes but are also frequently approached by nondominant castes for the settlement of their internal, even domestic, disputes.[82]

In nineteenth-century China, members of the gentry arbitrated many of the disputes of lower-status people.[83] Similarly, in medieval Europe, adjudicating the disputes of vassals was one of the most important peace-time functions of feudal lords; since one man's lord was often another man's vassal, there tended to be a rough upward movement of disputes from one status level to another that began at the bottom and worked its way to the top.[84] Certainly, few disputes in stratified societies are referred in a downward direction, to the consideration of social inferiors. Holding intimacy constant, peers play an intermediate role, but they have difficulty in imposing and enforcing their judgments.[85] Even where disputes with others are not at issue, but only the moral assessment of personal conduct, the status of outsiders is of crucial importance in determining their involvement. Thus, in Europe during the Middle Ages, the Christian sacrament of penance was administered so that people could tell their sins and seek absolution from those of equal status: Kings confessed to archbishops, dukes to bishops, barons to priests from the chief towns, and ordinary people to ordinary parish priests.[86] "These status regulations ensured that the sacrament of penance did not endanger or sabotage the hierarchy of feudal estates by requesting the nobility to confess to poor priests."[87] Given these patterns, for an individual to submit a strictly personal conflict—such as a domestic dispute—to a third party who is of no higher standing than himself or herself is an act of deference at odds with social realities. This is especially a liability for third parties who—like the police in contemporary society—are by their role fundamentally coercive in their approach to the problems they handle. Any hesitancy people might have in bringing peers, much less subordinates, into their domestic or other intimate tensions is multiplied considerably when those people are in a position to exercise authority over them. Finally, higher-status intimates will probably hesitate to use third parties all the more if, like judges, their business is conducted in public, where people of lower status may witness the proceedings.

It is consistent with all of this that higher-status disputants in a number of settings are less willing than others to invoke a variety of third parties. Thus, one study of the police in three large American cities found that cases initiated by lower-status people more often pertain to disputes between family members and other intimates than do cases initiated by higher-status people.[88] Along similar lines, higher-status women in Kentucky are less likely to contact the police or ministers about domestic violence than lower-status women are,[89] and, in Levittown (a suburb of Philadelphia and Trenton), domestic disputes which come to the attention of the police involve mostly working-class people.[90] More generally, there is reason to believe that a large proportion of all cases heard in criminal courts arise from domestic disputes, and yet higher-status defendants are strikingly absent from these courtrooms.[91] Another study, this one of civil commitment proceedings, provides further evidence, concluding that involuntary commitment of those seen as mentally ill (something usually sought by a family member) "is used primarily by the poor and the lower-middle class. Seldom do middle-class or upper-class persons bring petitions against one of their own."[92] Similarly, it has been observed that among the Zapotec Indians of Mexico,

> certain classes of people avoid using the courts. For example, the families of the *principales*, the leading government advisers, rarely utilize the town court. . . . For any member of such a respected or respectable family to be found in court would be considered a shame, and any wise member of such a family hesitates before involving the name of his family in a public hearing.[93]

Examining the situation in Hampton in these terms, it becomes significant that the majority of people there—those of the middle class—are generally equal or superior in social standing to all available third parties. Members of the working-class population, while ranking below some of the more formal agents of social control in income and prestige, are also equal to most of those who might play a role in their affairs (their neighbors, for example, or the police). Furthermore, the economic independence and autonomy that they, like middle-class people, experience on a daily basis, undermine their willingness to subordinate themselves in any context. The prevailing absence of significantly higher-status persons thus leaves all people with a greatly restricted number of acceptable third parties. At the same time, what status differences do exist find expression in the fact that it is women, young people, and working-class people—all of somewhat lower standing—who turn to third parties most often. Status dynamics also help to account for the indirect fashion in which many of those middle-class people who do invoke third parties go about it—notably, by calling upon a therapist for help because of personal emotional problems rather than admitting a conflict openly. The impact of status, combined with the effects of social distance, can thus explain why third parties have so little to do with Hampton's domestic conflicts.

· · ·

Hampton's families, then, appear to exercise relatively restrained and minimalistic responses to grievances for a variety of reasons, including their isolation and status in the wider community and their internal independence, autonomy, and atomization. Many of these characteristics are even more pronounced, however, in the relationships that prevail between friends and neighbors. There, an even lesser degree of social cohesiveness produces even weaker responses to disapproved behavior.

4

The Moral Order of Friendships and Neighborhoods

More than anything else, it is the moral order prevailing in Hampton's neighborhoods and friendship networks that gives the town its special character. An air of harmony, tranquillity, and civility results in large part from the restrained manner in which people deal with offensive acquaintances beyond their homes. In general, the town's residents favor nonconfrontational strategies of conflict management in this context: tolerating conduct they regard as deviant and taking no counteraction, simply avoiding offenders, approaching offenders in a conciliatory fashion and seeking an accommodation, or, less often, forwarding secret complaints to officials. As a consequence, friends and neighbors experience few open disputes, and social control between them is rarely noticed by anyone who is not directly involved. Moral minimalism prevails in Hampton's neighborhoods even more than in its families.

The techniques favored in this suburb, which entail little or no confrontation and which cope with conflict by stifling or denying it, differ dramatically from those found in many other settings. They exclude, for instance, the violence seen in the feuds, duels, and other acts of vengeance common in some groups—such as the Kapauku and Jalé of New Guinea, the Jivaro of Ecuador and Peru, the Yano-

This chapter is a revised version of a paper entitled "Social Control in Suburbia," which appeared in *Toward a General Theory of Social Control*, Vol. 2: *Selected Problems*, edited by Donald Black (Orlando: Academic Press, 1984), pp. 79–103. Copyright © 1984 by Academic Press, Inc.

mamö of Brazil, the Nuer of the Sudan, the Somali of Somalia, and aristocratic Europeans of an earlier time.[1] Simultaneously, they leave out the full airings of mutual dissatisfaction seen in the moots and negotiation sessions of many people, including the Kpelle of Liberia, the Tiv of Nigeria, the Arusha of Tanzania, the Tibetan nomads, the ancient Germans, and numerous others.[2] As in the town's families, the atomization, transiency, and fragmentation of social ties in Hampton's friendships and neighborhoods encourage unusually minimal responses to grievances. Since these traits are more extreme outside the family than within it, the moral order of the larger community is even more noteworthy for its calm.

Conflict Management without Confrontation

Hampton's citizens are quick to note that, unlike New York City, theirs is a community in which people "get along" and "don't kill each other." It is nonetheless the case that grievances arise with regularity. This is so despite the fact that tensions seem to be minimized in the first place by the extensive freedom of association and the pervasive privacy that characterize suburban—and especially middle-class suburban—life, features which allow people to restrict many of their dealings to those with whom they feel compatible.[3] Barking dogs, rambunctious children, untended yards, perceived insults and encroachments, and a variety of other annoyances and offenses are common throughout the town. No one can escape experiences of this kind completely, and though, like the great majority of grievances everywhere, they are quite mundane and trivial to an outsider, they can also be very bothersome and consequential for the people involved. When confronted with problems such as these, Hampton's suburbanites have several typical responses.

Everyday Conflict Management

In Hampton, doing nothing more than grumbling privately to family members or close friends is the most common strategy of conflict management. This study recorded dozens of idle complaints that were unaccompanied by any more positive action. Other investigators have labeled this type of response "lumping it" or "endurance,"[4] though in Hampton many grievances seem to be quickly forgotten rather than suffered as those labels might suggest. In any event, most people bear with diverse annoyances most of the time and, as a result, avoid the risk of becoming embroiled in conflict. This is especially true of the middle class. Rather than take decisive action, they will tolerate much conduct that greatly disturbs or offends them.

Thus, for example, a woman did nothing about her next-door neighbor's huge stacks of rotting and fungus-encrusted wood, even though she found them unsightly and perceived them as dangerous to her health. She merely remarked to relatives that "Barney [the neighbor] has a mental illness about wood," and described in detail the diseases she felt she might contract because of him. In a mixed-class neighborhood, most people similarly took no action against a man who periodically burned chicken feathers and droppings accumulated in his poultry shop, although the stench created—similar to that of burning hair—was extremely offensive to them and persisted for hours at a time. One family simply ignored the exhibitionistic antics of a man who lived next to them:

> The Shepards were a middle-class family who always got along well with people during their years in Hampton. They were disturbed, however, by the fact that one of their next-door neighbors was prone to exhibitionism. The offender in this matter was a middle-aged man who lived with his sister. Upon one occasion, for example, he arrived at the Shepards' door completely naked, rang the bell, and told a startled Mrs. Shepard and her children that he just wanted to return some mail of theirs mistakenly delivered to his address. Mrs. Shepard simply took the mail. Another time, the man woke Mr. and Mrs. Shepard early one weekend morning by throwing pebbles at their bedroom window, all the while dancing naked around his yard. The Shepards chose to ignore him. The man was also observed defecating on his lawn by one of the Shepard girls and her friends. (The girls felt certain that the neighbor waited to be sure he was seen before engaging in this act.) Through all these incidents, the Shepard family continued to be amiable toward the offender. Mrs. Shepard did once remark that they "really ought to see about getting that poor

man some help," but in fact they did nothing at all. They also continued to socialize with the man's sister, for whom they reportedly felt sympathy. The situation finally resolved itself when the exhibitionist and his sister moved away.

Another family learned that their neighbors had been aggravated for years by spotlights they had installed, which shone into the neighbor's home, only when they themselves requested a public hearing before a town agency on an unrelated matter. At this hearing, one of their neighbors mentioned the offending lights. People bore with such annoyances as loud rock music, dissonant trumpet practice, an unchained St. Bernard which ran loose and slobbered on those it encountered, a dog bite inflicted on a child by a neighbor's pet, and injuries to children caused by other children, among assorted problems.

The rarity of confrontation does not merely result from the fact that numerous deviants are allowed to escape sanctioning, however. Even when people do respond to offenders, they generally do so obliquely rather than directly. Avoidance is a favorite tactic of social control. In practice, the transition from inaction to avoidance is nearly imperceptible, since the latter generally begins with little or no fanfare. Suburban people are rarely thrown together in the course of daily events. Even very amicable neighbors commonly pass days without encountering each other, and those who consider themselves good friends may likewise see one another only occasionally. A person or family who hardly knows the neighbors and has few friends attracts little attention, and isolation of this sort may not be noticed at all. If it is, and if it arouses comment, others are likely to say simply that the party in question "minds his [or her] own business." Where social life is so loosely structured, it is an easy matter to avoid dealing with anyone regarded as offensive or otherwise undesirable.

Among friends and neighbors, avoidance means that aggrieved parties do not greet offenders when they encounter them, or greet them only pefunctorily, do not invite them over or visit them, and do not offer them small favors or ask them for such. In fact, they make an effort not to see them at all. In their comments, middle-class Hamptonians indicate that they consider it a mark of maturity and responsibility to rely heavily upon avoidance as a way of dealing with bothersome people. It might be added that in the few cases in which individuals appeared in the municipal criminal court to press grievances against neighbors or other acquaintances, the judge usually recommended avoidance as the optimal way to manage the conflict.

Because neighborhoods and friendship networks tend to be atomized, especially among the middle class, people in Hampton rarely exercise avoidance collectively in the form of a boycott. When several people avoid a person or a family at the same time, this is generally the product of individual actions or the actions of small groups of friends, and little or no resentment is voiced about those who continue to associate with the offender. In many cases, in fact, people are not even aware of who has dealings with whom. Thus, in one neighborhood, many people independently avoided a family whose house was considered "filthy." Other problems were handled in a similar way:

> The Callaghans were an elderly couple who had lived in Hampton most of their lives. Though Mr. Callaghan had worked as a custodian, they resided in a middle-class neighborhood. From the point of view of most of their neighbors, they were a problem. The most outrageous practice of the Callaghans, as far as their neighbors were concerned, was their habit of sitting and drinking alcohol on their front porch during the course of any day that was neither too cold or rainy. These drinking sessions lasted for hours, and both Mr. and Mrs. Callaghan appeared to others to become drunk during them. Their conversation would become louder and louder, and they would begin to use profanity liberally. All of this especially bothered their neighbors because it was routinely done while young children were outside playing, free to observe the drinking and to overhear the "bad" language. In response to the Callaghans' conduct, their near neighbors began, one by one, to avoid them. They rarely chatted with the Callaghans, never invited them over, and generally ignored them. They also carefully instructed their children to stay away from the older couple and to have nothing to do with them. As a result, the Callaghans were very isolated in their own neighborhood. Many of those avoiding them, however, were unaware whether other neighbors had any dealings with them or not.

"Wacky" Wharton, as the young people of her neighborhood called her, was an eccentric old woman who lived alone in a large house on a middle-class street in Hampton. Her unconventional behavior alienated her from her neighbors. Perhaps what people minded the most was her habit of accosting any of them who happened to be available and chattering incessantly and aimlessly, refusing to terminate a conversation gracefully. Other unusual actions also disturbed her neighbors, however. On one occasion, several people heard loud noises coming from Mrs. Wharton's yard and stepped out of their houses to investigate. They discovered that the woman was throwing dishes out of a downstairs window. In addition, Mrs. Wharton was often observed striking matches for no apparent reason, blowing them out, and dropping them on the ground behind her by lifting one leg and tossing them beneath it. In one well-known escapade, she drove around a downtown flagpole for hours in order to dramatize a grievance she had against the police. The people who lived around Mrs. Wharton generally chose to avoid her. They almost never socialized with her, and many went to great pains to avoid running into her on the street. Since Mrs. Wharton seemed to enjoy talking to people, this may have spurred her to greater efforts to initiate conversation. Nonetheless, the avoidance exercised against her independently by many neighbors, who never organized a collective response and who remained largely ignorant of one another's actions, was extensive and prolonged, and severely cut her off from the community.

Avoidance may also be a response to a single incident:

Bob Zimmer, a teenager from a middle-class family, returned home after attending church one Sunday morning to find that his new stereo tapedeck was missing from his car. Since the car had been parked behind his house while he was away, it seemed most unlikely to him that someone had just happened upon it and stolen it opportunistically. After some reflection, he determined that a particular friend of his must have been responsible. He suspected this person, a youth of about the same age from a working-class family, for several reasons. For one thing, he had a long history of committing thefts and had been in trouble with the Hampton police on many occasions. Beyond this, he knew that young Zimmer had a tapedeck in his car and, at the time it disappeared, knew that everyone in the Zimmer household was temporarily away. Mr. and Mrs. Zimmer and Bob's brothers and sisters all agreed that his friend had undoubtedly taken the tapedeck. All of them (but especially the adults who had always had misgivings about this friendship) strongly urged Bob to terminate dealings with his friend in the future. Bob did so, thereafter having very little contact with a person who had once been a close associate. He never called the police to report the theft or his suspicions about it, however, nor did he confront his friend with accusations of any kind. In a classic case of avoidance, he simply altered the terms of the relationship drastically and without notice.

In another case, a middle-aged woman infuriated a friend by remarking, in the context of a discussion about incest, that she thought the friend secretly desired such a relationship with her son. The insulted woman responded with avoidance. Similarly, a family began to avoid a neighbor who had criticized their daughter's boyfriend.

Avoidance outside the family usually does not elicit intervention by third parties. On the contrary, people generally claim that those who do not get along *should* avoid each other. They also state that it is improper and unwise for outsiders to become embroiled in conflicts that do not directly impinge upon them. In practice, this means that one spouse may continue interacting amiably with a person whom the other spouse is avoiding. Several such cases came to light during this study, and appeared to arouse no special interest in the townspeople who knew of them. Since people are often hesitant to press a conflict openly, whether to escalation or to resolution, avoidance is an acceptable response which freezes hostilities and allows the parties involved to turn their attention elsewhere.

Despite the positive evaluation of avoidance as a way of coping with tensions, however, and despite its prevalence in practice, people in Hampton do sometimes opt to approach offenders directly in order to seek accommodations from them. While such an action is more forceful than tolerating a grievance or relying exclusively upon avoidance, it is still remarkable for the extent to which it occurs without open conflict, particularly where middle-class parties are concerned. Indeed, it is common for people to request satisfaction in such a way that they not only adopt a posture of reason and moderation but even appear to be asking a favor of the offender.

Conciliatory approaches of this kind are best described by example:

> In a middle-class neighborhood of Hampton, a man who had built a small ornamental pond in his yard which he stocked with goldfish was disturbed to discover that the fish died shortly after he bought them. He replaced the fish, but the second batch suffered the same fate. The man soon decided that his fish were being injured by the many neighborhood children who came to the pond to look at them and, on occasion, to poke at them with sticks or to throw rocks at them. He put up a "no trespassing" sign and asked his own children to discourage the visitors, but the pond continued to be an attraction and the goldfish continued to die. After some time, the man opted for a new tactic. He instructed his children to ask the names of all those found at pondside, whether they appeared to be injuring the fish or not, and then telephoned the parents of each. In these conversations, he explained his problem at some length and noted that he was on the verge of giving up on the fish altogether. He remarked that he did not know exactly which children might be causing the damage, and observed that in any case it was probably inadvertent rather than malicious. Finally, he asked the parents if they could possibly discourage their children from visiting the pond. The reactions of those he called were generally sympathetic, and all of the parents apparently instructed their youngsters to stay away from the man's yard. (It was not learned, however, whether this affected the well-being of the goldfish.)

> Mr. Treadwell, a middle-aged, middle-class man, had lived in his home for some time when a family with several teenaged boys moved in across the street. His new young neighbors, along with their friends, soon showed a tendency to congregate in a parking area at the back of their house, where they talked, played music, and occasionally drank beer. The traffic in and out of the driveway was heavy by neighborhood standards. Furthermore, many of the boys drove somewhat unrespectable vehicles—motorcycles, sports cars, "souped-up" trucks, etc.—and they also tended to drive fast and noisily, roaring in and out with their radios blaring and tires squealing. After doing nothing about the situation during the first summer following the boys' arrival, the man enjoyed a respite in the winter. But the next spring the problem resumed. Finally, Mr. Treadwell approached the boys' father one day when both men happened to be outside. He

remarked that his daughter would soon be home from college and that he was concerned that she or a friend of hers might be hit by one of the vehicles speeding in or out of the driveway across the street. He asked the other man if he would mention the problem to his sons, and urge them to drive more slowly in the future. The encounter was amiable, and the boys' father did in fact bring the matter up with his sons. They, for their part, despite observing that Mr. Treadwell's daughter must attend a "retard school" if she did not "know enough to get out of the way of a car," responded favorably to his request and asked their friends to be more conservative in their driving as well. After this, the two families became, if anything, more friendly with one another. The boys even shoveled their neighbor's snow as a favor the next winter.

Although they may grumble privately about receiving such complaints, most people approached in this way are willing to accommodate the aggrieved parties. If they are not, the complainants usually fall back upon tolerance or avoidance. When one of the many people subjected to the odor of burning chicken feathers, described previously, finally remarked jovially to the offender that she "hated the smell of burning chicken-do," the man to whom she voiced her complaint responded, also lightheartedly, "too bad." The woman then dropped the matter and continued to be friendly toward the offender.[5] Because those approached are generally cooperative, and because, when they are not, aggrieved persons tend not to press the issue, verbal altercations outside the family are uncommon.

Only in a relatively small number of cases do people in Hampton take their grievances to an official third party for action of some kind. The police, court personnel, zoning officers, sanitarians, and elected officials are all prepared to receive and process complaints from townspeople about each other. What is especially noteworthy in this context is not only that this tactic is infrequent, but that when it does occur, the complainants are very often at pains to remain unknown to the offenders. In many cases they even refuse to divulge their identities to the officials whom they contact.

People often make anonymous complaints despite a guarantee of confidentiality by the agency involved, as is the custom at the Zoning Office and the Board of Health. The police, too, take calls made anonymously and will often protect the identities of complainants who are known to them. (To the police, conflicts in Hampton are "touchy matters" to be handled with the utmost discretion.) Unlike the zoning officers and sanitarians, however, the police frequently inform citizens that they can take no action against an offender—beyond a warning—unless the aggrieved party steps forward publicly and signs a written complaint. This is necessary, by their account, for any misdemeanor not witnessed by an officer. As a result of this policy, many complainants abandon their efforts to involve the law and adopt such tactics as tolerance or avoidance. They would rather suffer their problems than confront the offenders openly.[6] Some voice resentment toward the police. One man, for instance, was still expressing indignation a year later that the officers who handled his complaint about neighborhood youths lighting firecrackers had asked him "to sign [his] life away" before they would take formal action.

People may also notify elected officials about interpersonal conflicts outside the family. Like the sanitarians, zoning officers, and police, these officials normally keep information about complainants to themselves—if they have it. Some citizens refuse to reveal their identities, even when pressed to leave their names so that they may be informed of actions taken on their behalf. Only the court, for purposes of its formal hearings, requires complainants to come forward publicly. It may be partly for this reason that the court is so underutilized as a means of social control.

Since it is not only from officials that the identities of complainants can be learned, but also from clues provided by the circumstances surrounding a complaint, factors other than guarantees of confidentiality appear to influence patterns of complaint. People are far more willing to contact an official about problems that affect everyone in a neighborhood indiscriminately—loud music, for example, or roaming dogs—than about annoyances clearly linked to themselves. In cases of the former kind it is difficult for offenders to infer who has complained against them. Such was true when a man called the police about the noise one of his neighbors was making with a power saw, when a woman complained to the police and the mayor about music from a nearby church, and when a man complained to a town council member and the zoning office about the illegal conversion of a private home in his neighborhood into several rental units. It was also true when someone made three separate complaints about a particular unleashed dog. In this instance, the dog's owner became increasingly frustrated because she could not pinpoint who the disgruntled neighbor was, something she wanted to know, she said, so that she might make peace with the unhappy individual.

Secret complaints both stifle and obscure hostility between the parties involved. People visited unexpectedly by a police officer, a zoning officer, or a sanitarian may be extremely angry, but as long as they are unable to direct their anger at a specific target they are generally unable to take any counteractions. Few retaliations, threatened or executed, can be aimed at neighborhoods in general. The complainant is even able to continue amicable dealings with the offender as if nothing had happened, while the hostility which generated the complaint remains hidden beneath an outward appearance of good will.

Infrequent Responses

The distinctive character of social control in Hampton is determined in large part by what is not done when people have grievances against their associates. Especially rare are tactics of social control entailing aggressive confrontation between the parties involved. In comparison with what happens in surrounding cities, assaults, serious threats, tire slashings, and such like incidents are rare. Few people carry or use such dangerous weapons as guns, switchblades, and razors, and no homicide between friends or neighbors has occurred in the town in the memory of its current residents. Violence and property destruction are especially uncommon among middle-class adults, who, for all intents and purposes, do not resort to them. The most aggressive action by such a person discovered during this study happened when a man who was disputing with a neighboring youth intentionally put his fingers on the latter's freshly waxed car. While young people and working-class people are somewhat more violent, in cross-cultural perspective they also appear remarkably peaceful.

For lack of opportunity if for no other reason, deprivations of anything but social interaction are also uncommon as a way to sanction offensive friends and neighbors. Individuals rarely have the means to punish such people by depriving them of valued resources or opportunities. Only one institution in the town provides an arena in which meaningful deprivations can easily be inflicted—the town's Zoning Board of Adjustment, which is called upon to grant exceptions ("variances") to individuals who wish to be released from prohibitions in the zoning ordinances. (These requests may arise from building projects that would violate space requirements or from a desire to expand a building's use—for instance, to add an apartment where it would be prohibited.) Technically, applicants for a variance are required to demonstrate "hardship" by showing that a refusal would impose an unfair burden upon them. In practice, the definition of hardship is fluid and a great deal of discretion rests with the Zoning Board members. Decisions appear to be heavily influenced by the attitudes of an applicant's neighbors, who are required to be notified of any variance request.

During the first half of 1978, the Zoning Board considered 19 petitions for variances; in 7 of these cases, neighbors voiced either strong approval or disapproval of the request. (In all other cases, Zoning Board members assumed tacit support, since they always formally invite neighbors to step forward with any objections.) Although most variance requests are successful, in every instance in which neighbors voiced opposition to an application (a total of 5 cases), they succeeded in hindering it to some degree— either stopping it altogether (in 3 cases) or at least winning some modification as a sort of compromise (in 2 cases). Most of the disapproving neighbors had experienced earlier conflict with the applicants.

Not visible in these figures are cases in which hostile neighbors may have had an impact behind the scenes. The secretary to the Zoning Board counsels people that they may experience difficulties with an application if she becomes aware of conflict between them and their neighbors. In one case, she informed a family who wanted to build an addition to their home that the hard feelings caused by their six dogs would be a problem should they petition for a variance. It is difficult to estimate how often considerations of this kind affect the decision to seek a variance, but the zoning officer calculates that presently only half of the people whose building plans necessitate a variance decide to seek one, while the others simply change their minds about their projects. On the other hand, it is also unclear from the available evidence how many neighbors who feel ill-will towards applicants nonetheless keep silent and allow their requests to be approved.

In any event, opposing a neighbor's variance request is a rare and opportunistic sanction, one which few people are ever in a position to employ. Spiteful deprivations in other contexts are even rarer. The mutual independence of suburbanites renders most of them immune to punishments of this kind.

Also uncommon are attempts to impose psychotherapy or other therapeutic social control upon offending friends or neighbors. In one of the few such cases during this study neighbors mobilized the social workers at the Board of Health to obtain help for a woman who was, in their opinion, abusing children left in her care during the day. In another case, a group of non-Italian women tried to convince an Italian immigrant to accept money from their club to send his twelve-year-old son to camp. They argued that the boy was suffering emotionally from spending as much time as he did with his father, whom he accompanied to work whenever possible. (The father was a sexton at a church in town.) When the man grew angry and insisted that the women leave him alone, they dropped the matter, although they commented among themselves about his rudeness and the damage the boy was sustaining. The infrequency of efforts to impose therapeutic help is all the more noteworthy because people in the town often discuss conflict in psychological terms.

Equally unusual are gatherings devoted to the mediation or negotiation of disputes. Nothing more elaborate than the conciliatory approaches already described occurs with any regularity, and people rarely convene in any forum to have a complete airing of disagreements or to arrive at explicit reconciliations. There are no places—like the beerhalls of Bavaria, the coffeehouses of the Near East, or the homes of prominent citizens in rural Ireland[7]—where individuals have their grievances weighed and processed by groups of interested associates. Nor do individuals seek to hold meetings for such a purpose; moots such as those found in Europe during the tribal period or in parts of Africa do not occur.[8] Similarly, people rarely call upon members of the clergy to mediate conflicts involving nonfamily members. Even extensive dyadic negotiations involving principals alone are infrequent. This applies in friendships and even more so in other relationships. Finally, it should be observed that formal legal contests are rare as well. During forty weekly sessions of the town's municipal criminal court held in 1978 and 1979, only 27 cases were initiated by friends, neighbors, or acquaintances. Since private prosecution is the norm in this court, the bringing of legal actions ordinarily involves a great deal of confrontation. People appear to be more at ease when the police and prosecutor handle their complaints, but the circumstances under which anyone is likely to receive this service—notably when predatory strangers such as burglars are apprehended and tried in a higher court—are uncommon. On the civil side, only one case involving friends or neighbors was uncovered.

In sum, one feature of social control among Hamptonians, especially those of the middle class, is an absence of confrontation. This is a part of the pervasive moral minimalism that exists in the suburb, with residents typically taking little action when offended. Such nonconfrontation contrasts with what occurs in many other communities throughout the world, where people air their conflicts more openly and prosecute their grievances more forcefully. Not all of the residents of Hampton are equally unlikely, however, to confront offenders. In seeking to explain patterns of social control, it is important to observe which segments of the town's population are most inclined to employ direct tactics when they experience problems with others.

Variations

To a large extent, young people and working-class people in Hampton favor the same modes of social control as middle-class adults do. Nonetheless, it is possible to discern a tendency in both groups toward a greater reliance upon confrontation. Age and

social class interact in this regard, so that working-class youths are
the most likely of all Hamptonians to adopt an aggressive posture
toward their adversaries. In fact, it is only in this group that hostile
confrontation is a somewhat prominent strategy of social control.

Age

Among young people, particularly those from working-class families, physical aggression occurs with some frequency—though it is
rarely of a sort to cause serious injury, and virtually never involves
weapons. For example, on weekend nights at local bars brief
altercations commonly occur between drunk patrons who know
one another before the fights take place. Bar employees and other
customers handle most of these incidents by themselves, without
the help of the police.

Fights occur spontaneously in other settings as well. Some are
prearranged and have a ritualized character. In these cases, word
of an impending confrontation circulates rapidly through the
disputants' social networks, and the conflict becomes subject to
the regulation of peers. If they approve the fight and make no
effort to stop it, members of this "public" will appear as observers,
bringing with them group standards of justice and fair play. They
decide when a fight should be stopped and who has won, and they
oversee what techniques are used and the degree of violence
inflicted. It appears that this supervision keeps the level of injury
low.

Young people also issue many more personal threats than
older people, and they engage in more harassment and more
property destruction as forms of punishment. In one case, a young
man drove his car onto a neighbor's lawn during the course of a
conflict; in another, a group of young friends retaliated for an
affront to one of their number by driving past the offender's house
late at night while blowing their car horns; in a third case, young
people left a bag of manure on the doorstep of an unpopular
neighbor. When a man called the police to disperse a group of
young neighbors who were sitting in cars drinking and listening to
music, they responded by spraying the sides of his house with black
spray paint during the middle of the night. In fact, much "vandal-

ism" in the town is property destruction undertaken by young people as a form of social control.[9]

Finally, young men in Hampton are overrepresented among those who press formal complaints, particularly those heard in the municipal criminal court. It is also relevant to note that the only civil action involving friends or neighbors occurred when one youth sued another to recover a $400 debt—an action that was criticized by the older people who learned of it.

Social Class

Working-class adults are more likely than middle-class adults to opt for confrontation. Violence, for example, though much less common than among youths, is still found, and several incidents involving fights and property destruction between adults in the working-class community were uncovered in this study. In one case, an altercation broke out between two groups of men when one faction installed a "spite fence" down the middle of a shared driveway. During the encounter, one man sustained a broken nose and several car windows were smashed. In another case, two friends and co-workers exchanged blows over who should win a union election. Fisticuffs and damage to automobiles occurred in other instances as well, and once two women scuffled after Sunday Mass until they were separated by a priest. The initial aggressor in this matter accused the other woman of having an affair with her husband.[10]

Formal complaints are dominated by working-class people, too, even though much accepted wisdom about the use of law would predict the opposite.[11] The police report that "blue-collar" people more frequently call them into disputes that are "civil matters" and "not strictly police business," usually code words for disputes between people in preexistent relationships.[12] Consistent with this, in the present study the majority of calls to the police about neighbors originated with working-class people, though they constitute only about a third of the town's population. Working-class people not only appear to call the police more often about their own affairs, but also about the conflicts of their working-class neighbors and friends.

The greater willingness of working-class people to resort to law against friends and neighbors can be seen in the municipal court. There, about 60 percent of the 27 cases between friends and neighbors observed during this study involved two working-class people. Another 15 percent were brought by working-class individuals against those of middle-class status. The same pattern appears in the administrative realm. The chief zoning officer reported being struck by the large number of complaints brought by Italian-Americans (the largest segment of the town's working class). He said that "most" of his cases originate with this ethnic group. The chief sanitarian also observed that most of his cases begin with complaints from Italian-American people, and noted that individuals from the most exclusive section of town "never" bring complaints against their neighbors. Information was obtained about 18 specific conflicts taken to the two agencies (8 to the Zoning Office, 9 to the Board of Health, and 1 to both). Eleven of these, or about 60 percent, involved working-class neighbors, the remaining 7, or about 40 percent, involved middle-class people—once again an overrepresentation of the working class and an underrepresentation of the middle class. For each agency separately as well, most of the complaints came from working-class people.

Finally, it might be pointed out that working-class people are also more likely than middle-class people to complain to elected officials about their neighbors. Eleven, or about two-thirds, of the 16 complaints to the mayor or town council members included in this study originated with working-class people. In fact, only the civil court—used by just one set of friends in all the cases gathered—constituted an exception to the pattern.

It is important in this context to emphasize that the kinds of problems which working-class people bring to official third parties do not appear to be so unusually prevalent among them that they can account for a higher complaint rate. The most common neighbor problem aired in the municipal court was an obnoxious dog—something which, in everyday life, plagues middle-class people just about as often as working-class people. Similarly, the occasions for contacting zoning officers and sanitarians are widely dispersed throughout Hampton's population. Grievances actually brought include excessive noise (in one case from a young neighbor's motorcycle, in another from a neighbor's trucks), offensive smells, apartments and businesses in areas zoned against them, bothersome animals, and unsightly recreational trailers parked in people's driveways. While neighbors with trucks are more likely to be found in working-class areas, most of the other situations occur with essentially equal frequency throughout the town. One man complained to the Zoning Office that his neighbor's swimming pool was too close to the road. Another cited a neighbor for building without a permit—the structure in question turned out to be a treehouse. Two women who lived near each other in a garden-apartment complex accused one another of violating the health code—the first (called the "bird lady" by the sanitarians) objected to the other's numerous cats which, she claimed, eliminated their waste in her flower beds, while the second (the "cat lady") retaliated by complaining that the bird lady threw leftover spaghetti and other garbage onto her lawn for birds to eat. Finally, elected officials too hear about problems of a sort that arise throughout the population—noisy neighbors, allegedly unkempt houses and houselots, even unruly children. One man called the mayor twice on a single weekend to complain that his neighbor's recent property improvements now caused water to accumulate on his (the complainant's) front lawn. Another man approached a member of the town council to express displeasure that the teenaged daughter of one of his neighbors was dating a black youth. In general, then, while all segments of the town experience many grievances of a sort that might be submitted to the consideration of an official, working-class people choose this alternative more often. Their disproportionate use of official agents of social control, as well as other kinds of confrontation, has helped to create for Hampton's Italian-American working class a local reputation as a "feuding culture."

·   ·   ·

The greater willingness of young and working-class people to pursue offenders openly suggests that the generally low use of confrontative tactics in Hampton is related to features of social life most pronounced in the adult middle class. At the same time,

all people in Hampton have much in common and no group stands
out as very confrontational in light of cross-cultural patterns. The
discussion that follows attempts to account for the town's low
levels of open conflict and aggression in terms of the distinctive
social dynamics found most especially among grown-up members
of the middle-class majority. It is important to bear in mind,
however, that what is said is often true for the rest of the town as
well, insofar as other people share the social experiences of middle-class adults.

Weak Ties and Moral Minimalism

Two characteristics most clearly distinguish middle-class friends
and neighbors and reverberate across many dimensions of their
lives. These are their high social status and the structure of their
personal relationships. In the same ways in which these factors
promote moral minimalism in families, they do so in friendships
and neighborhoods. Thus, one effect of social status is that it
discourages the involvement of a third party. Since few outsiders
have status sufficiently superior to command deference and respect, few are consulted about interpersonal tensions. A recent
study of a Bavarian village found, for example, that comparatively
high-status people—those with secure incomes and standing in
the community—initiated suits against peers in the court or the
so-called "reconciliation agency" far less than those of low-status
did.[13] Similarly, when King Louis XIV of France attempted to
discourage dueling by setting up a "court of honor" where aristocrats could air their grievances against one another and receive
judgments, his experiment failed because nobles refused to use the
court.[14] Yet, to explain the strong aversion to confrontation of all
kinds among the middle class of Hampton in terms of social status
alone seems inadequate.

The annals of history and anthropology contain many refer-
ences to a propensity for frequent and forceful prosecution of
grievances by high-status people. Thus, for example, in at least one
area in India, disputes among high-caste individuals are said to

have been "frequent, bitter and often violent. . . . These fights would often be over questions of land, but more frequently would arise over insults."[15] Among the Nuristani of Afghanistan, informants report that aggression and attendant mediation are more common among high-status people than among lower-status ones, who are said to be less likely to quarrel.[16] Similarly, in a contemporary Lebanese village, members of the highest stratum "have more disputes than the other social classes," partly since they are "quick to take affront for any real or imagined slight to personal or lineage honor or position."[17] In medieval Europe, the nobility often answered offenses—which they too were quite ready to perceive—with violence. Thus, in one instance, "Perigord [a part of France] ran with blood because a certain lord thought that one of his noble neighbors looked like a blacksmith and had the bad taste to say so."[18] It therefore seems that social status, though an important influence upon moral life, does not by itself ensure the use of minimalistic strategies of conflict management.

A factor that seems more clearly to influence the predominance of nonconfrontation in the moral life of middle-class friends and neighbors in the suburbs is the morphology of their social relationships. Middle-class people tend to be socially anchored only loosely into their atomized and shifting networks of associates. Their high rate of mobility from place to place means that bonds between persons are frequently ruptured and replaced with new and equally temporary ones, so that relationships often have short pasts and futures. Even relatives (other than nuclear family members) are likely to reside elsewhere, at a distance too far for easy contact except by telephone. Middle-class lives are also highly compartmentalized. Relationships tend to be single-stranded, restricted to one dimension of interaction, and partly as a result, middle-class social networks are not interconnected and are not formed into dense webs of common associates. Ties are scattered through many regions and towns. In general, then, the world of middle-class suburbanites is one of "weak ties," in which people have assorted contacts rather than intimate relationships with many people.[19]

A culture of weak ties seems to undermine confrontation and promote moral minimalism in several ways: (1) it renders forceful action against antagonists less compelling by holding out the likelihood that a subsequent departure of either party will take care of the problem in the normal course of events, while it meanwhile makes avoidance a feasible option; (2) such a social order also makes bitter enmities and resentments difficult to sustain and limits the ability of people to accumulate damaging information about one another, partly by keeping offenses relatively private and out of the public view; (3) a system of weak ties lessens involvement in any single relationship and leaves people little time to manage conflicts within it; and (4) it deprives people of cohesive bands of allies or other supporters to assist them in pressing grievances, whether through violence or negotiation. In practice, these implications generally coexist and appear to be cumulative in their effects.

The Transiency of Problems

Especially for members of the middle class, the town of Hampton is often a temporary place of residence. Many transfer to other locations at their employers' request. Some take advantage of their considerable affluence to leave for personal reasons, usually to improve upon their dwelling or neighborhood. Still others take up new homes upon retirement, perhaps near one or more of their scattered children, or in a warmer climate. Only a few middle-class people seem committed to spending the rest of their lives in the same town, much less in the same neighborhood or house.

When a grievance arises, therefore, many friends and neighbors are able to look forward to eventual separation from the annoying situation. Even if the aggrieved individual is not likely to move, the chances are good that the offender will. Ordinary changes of residence do tend to truncate conflicts. In one instance, a middle-class woman about to move to another state (because her husband had been transferred) remarked that one of the best things about the move was that it would enable her to get away from a friend with whom she had been having intermittent disagreements for some time. In the case of the exhibitionist described earlier, the problem was ultimately resolved when the offender moved. And a neighborhood terrorized by an unruly St. Bernard was relieved when the dog's owners left town. The possibility of a graceful exit from a tense situation makes confrontation less compelling. People can opt for a holding pattern of tolerance or avoidance without having to submit to a permanent source of displeasure. This is a luxury not afforded to people everywhere in American society; the less affluent may be financially unable to move and may so be forced to choose between resignation or confrontation when tensions arise.[20]

At the same time, the loosely woven texture of life in Hampton makes avoidance on an everyday basis an easy alternative should an aggrieved person choose to take any action at all against an offending neighbor or friend. There is little pressure to associate with particular individuals, and few occasions are likely to bring together those who would rather stay apart. The sheer spatial arrangement of the town, with most families segregated on their private lots, makes avoidance easy. If tensions escalate, the parties can simply ignore one another without disrupting a larger network of associates. In many cases, their avoidance will not even be noticed.

As discussed above, evidence from other societies indicates that transient and atomized people everywhere are comparatively unlikely to confront offenders directly. The alternative of avoidance defuses many conflicts. Thus, accusations of witchcraft are less common in fluid and transient societies where people can simply move away from one another.[21] Violence too is less likely where avoidance is possible; recall, for example, that there was a dramatic increase in rates of violence among a traditionally nomadic people—the Chenchu of the Indian subcontinent—after they were confined by the British to a single enclosed camp.[22] Similarly, avoidance—in which people "no longer speak" to one another and refuse to drink at the same bar or to participate in the same activity—has been credited with the restraint of violence in an Italian village.[23] It has been hypothesized that mediation and adjudication will also be relatively undeveloped where it is possible for people to avoid their antagonists,[24] and a decline of law under contemporary conditions has been projected on the basis of the decreasing lifespan of relationships and a corresponding decrease in the lifespan of disputes.[25] Patterns of social control in Hampton are consistent with all of this.

The Scarcity of Information

Confrontation is further undermined and moral minimalism further encouraged by the scarcity of social knowledge involved in middle-class relationships. Of special interest in this context is the difficulty in accumulating information about any individual's past misdeeds, and the implications this has for the dynamics of reputation, or "normative status."[26] Direct experience with the same offender is apt to be limited by the tendency of people to move away from one another and by the low intensity of social bonds. Beyond this, the structure of relationships greatly reduces the amount of second-hand information people acquire about the behavior of others. When people move, their knowledge and opinions move as well. And even on a day-by-day basis, the low cohesiveness of social networks discourages the pooling of grievances and the sharing of compromising information. Accordingly, when a friend, neighbor, or associate annoys an individual, the problem is likely to appear as a first or second offense committed by a person with no particular reputation for good or ill. In fact, people hardly have reputations at all.

The relative absence of reputations in suburbia is quite significant, since first and second offenders everywhere appear to fare better than those who are seen as chronic deviants.[27] People tolerate first offenders more readily and, if they do sanction them, treat them more leniently than repeat offenders. This is true across societies and types of social control.[28] One anthropologist explains litigiousness in an African society in terms of the accumulation of grievances between parties over time.[29] Another explains execution, banishment, and witchcraft accusations in various societies in terms of the ability of the inhabitants to assemble "community dossiers" on one another; where social conditions make such dossiers impossible, sanctions of this kind are not prevalent.[30]

At the same time, where information about people is restricted, aggrieved parties are under little pressure to preserve
their "honor," or public reputations, by taking action against offenders anyway.[31] A concern with honor—which typically dictates
forceful retaliation for many offenses, including revenge slay-
ings—presupposes an audience who will know about the affairs of
others and whose opinions matter. In settings where this concern
exists, people demonstrate their worth and integrity to their fellows by refusing to tolerate mistreatment. Those who absorb
offenses which honor demands they avenge shame themselves
greatly. An anthropologist who has studied the dynamics of honor
concludes:

> [T]he important position accorded to sentiment of honour is a char-
> acteristic of "primary" societies in which the relationship with others,
> through its intensity, intimacy, and continuity, takes precedence over
> the relationship one has with oneself. . . . In groups whose members
> are well-known to each other, . . . the control of public opinion is
> exercised at every moment, and community feeling is experienced
> with the highest possible intensity. Penned inside this enclosed mi-
> crocosm in which everybody knows everybody, condemned without
> the possibility of escape or relief to live with others, beneath the gaze
> of others, every individual experiences deep anxiety about "people's
> words."[32]

The situation in the suburbs is far different. There, practially no
one knows what offenses occur or what responses they meet. Cut
off from others, living lives of extreme privacy and free of the
social pressure that a cohesive group of associates might provide,
people can handle their problems without regard to public opinion. Suburbanites have little or no honor to defend, and this helps
to explain why they take so little action in the face of grievances.

The Division of Social Attention

Because of the fragmentation of their social networks, middle-class
suburbanites experience considerable discontinuity from one interaction to the next. A husband and wife with whom another couple
exchanges visits are unlikely to have the same configuration of

contacts and interests as a bridge partner, a fellow club member, or a neighbor. Accordingly, each relationship provides its own activities and entails its own demands. Since people thus divide their social attention into many segments, comparatively little time and effort can be devoted to any one involvement.

This fragmentation of social attention, fostered in part by frequent activities away from home, supports the common claim of middle-class people that they are "too busy to be bothered" or "have no time" to pursue a grievance, or that they "have more to do than worry about" any given offensive associate. Other concerns—including those that are work-related—draw people away from the social settings in which their grievances arise. The more this is so, the less time remains to plan and execute sanctions against any offender, and the more conflicts of any sort are perceived as unwelcome intrusions that might interfere with other involvements.

This state of affairs may be contrasted with that prevailing in small, bonded groups. There, little is likely to be of more interest to everyone than interpersonal tensions between two or more members. With no outside involvements to distract their attention beyond the group, conflict can readily become a consuming preoccupation. It can also serve as a relief from unchanging interactions and unvarying routines, even becoming a source of entertainment. Thus, one investigator has noted for a closely connected and highly litigious Philippine society that

> in some respects, a Lipay trial is more comparable to an American poker game than to our legal proceedings. It is a contest of skill, in this case of verbal skill accompanied by social merry-making, in which the loser pays a forfeit. He pays for much the same reason we pay a poker debt: so he can play the game again.[33]

It might be added that conflict, whether entertainment or not, seems especially absorbing in groups which have few scheduled activities on a daily basis. In other words, there seems to be a tendency for conflict to expand to fill the time available. So, for example, both aristocrats in traditional societies and contemporary "juvenile delinquents" have little or no gainful employment—

both, in fact, enjoy a leisurely existence—and both often value and exploit violence in interpersonal relations.[34] To some extent, the same correlation can be found among chronically unemployed or underemployed adults in industrialized societies, for it is in such groups that rates of homicide and assault are highest.[35] Whether leisure results from choice or is forced upon people, then, it may have the effect of increasing moral confrontations, particularly if in providing time for socializing it brings about or increases intense relationships among a cohesive group of associates. In any event, the residents of Hampton, who fill their days with a great diversity of activities and people, often seem too distracted to follow up on their grievances and certainly fail to relish the drama of social conflict.

The Lack of Support

Weak ties also discourage confrontation and promote moral minimalism by depriving people of allies and other supporters. When tensions erupt, individuals are generally left to their own devices. Extended family members, who might otherwise be expected to lend assistance, are usually living some distance away and are, in any case, caught up in their own networks and concerns. Spouses and children are typically the only relatives present, and they too have other preoccupations (besides being, in the case of young children, of limited value in confrontations). Friends, neighbors, and other associates are near at hand but are rarely intimate enough to be relied upon. Even advice is difficult to obtain from those who know little or nothing about a problem, and many people are reluctant to give it under any circumstances (believing it preferable not to get involved in others' conflicts at all).

Without supporters to help in the management of their conflicts, people are more likely to forego direct confrontations. Evidence from nonsuburban settings indicates a close relationship between the availability of support and the vigorous prosecution of grievances. In one cross-cultural survey, for example, it was found that societies in which kin members are clustered into tightly knit "fraternal interest groups" tend to experience high levels of violent retaliation for injuries; those lacking such groups tend to be peaceful.[36] The relationship between social support and other kinds of direct confrontation has also been noted. Whether and to what extent disputes will be settled by negotiation, for example, depends greatly on the ability of the aggrieved parties to recruit an "action-set" to help them.[37] Resort to law also appears to be encouraged by the presence of support groups.[38] In ancient Athens, fraternities and clubs which assisted their members in legal matters—and to which "practically every Athenian of consequence belonged"—stimulated recourse to professional advocates and trials.[39] Hence, the absence of support groups in suburbia deters people from engaging in confrontations with their adversaries. Hampton's moral minimalism is partly understandable in this light.

•   •   •

This analysis helps to explain the greater propensity of young and working-class people to confront friends and neighbors who offend them. Along several dimensions of social morphology, each group differs from middle-class adults in ways that generate a more aggressive posture. Young people tend to move within the confines of more closely bonded networks and to develop more intense enmities as well as warmer friendships. With fewer far-flung ties, they are less divided in their interests and commitments and less distracted from their conflicts. A striking feature of the youthful response to grievances is the tendency of bands of good friends to rally around one another, so that hostility passes between groups. (Middle-class adults who, because of their more atomized networks, do not proceed collectively in the face of grievances are made somewhat uneasy by this fact. They fear that antagonizing one youth might provoke a "gang of kids" to exact vengeance.)

Working-class people are better organized for confrontation as well. Since they are less transient than middle-class people, their grievances are more permanent. They have a greater opportunity to accumulate grudges, and their more cohesive networks are able to collect, store, collate, and disseminate damaging information more efficiently. Like those of youths, their social lives are somewhat less fragmented, and they have fewer far-flung demands to distract them from their conflicts. Moreover, working-class people more often live near their extended families, and so they enjoy more dependable support.

For all these reasons, one would expect Hampton's youths and working-class people to engage in more aggressive and open conflict than middle-class adults—and they do. At the same time, the degree of variation in social relationships across segments of the town is actually quite limited when seen against the range found throughout human populations and even in more diverse American communities. In the matter of social status, for instance, working-class Hamptonians live lives largely free of the invidiousness that has been the lot of many—such as slaves, serfs, and peasants—the world around. Working-class consumption patterns compare favorably with those of the middle class, most working-class people own their own homes, and most work at jobs which require skill and which they find satisfying. Many are self-employed. Working-class people are not dependent on middle-class people, nor are they subject to their authority. On a day-by-day basis, then, working-class people in Hampton are not directly subordinated to their middle-class fellows. Since third parties who play a role in the conflicts of others tend to emerge from the ranks of the socially dominant, this degree of equality helps to explain why most working-class townspeople prefer to handle interpersonal tensions on their own. Like middle-class people, though to a lesser extent, those of the working class find sufficiently superordinate third parties in short supply.

In their social morphology as well, working-class residents and young people have much in common with middle-class adults. In the light of all human experience, both the working class and the young are themselves characterized by considerable transiency, atomization, and fragmentation in their social life. They too are drawn into a variety of segregated social contacts that divide their social involvements and create barriers to the accumulation of overlapping and damaging moral information. For them as for middle-class adults, it is largely possible simply to avoid interaction with antagonists, since most personal contact is voluntary. Neither working-class adults nor young people are embedded in especially large or organized support groups that would, in the manner of many tribal clans, incite and follow them into violent confrontations. (In this connection, it is significant that Hampton's working-class families are not particularly powerful, as families go.) The working class and young people—especially the latter, if they are middle class—experience considerable residential mobility, if only across town, and this also undercuts hostilities. In many ways, then, the people of Hampton are socially similar and understandably have much in common when they handle grievances.

• • •

In sum, the suburb of Hampton is a community of people who are, by world standards, remarkably autonomous, individuated, and transient. Its middle-class residents are especially so. The pattern of moral life found under these conditions is largely nonconfrontative, and indeed even weak. Moral minimalism prevails, with few grievances ever giving rise to full-scale conflict. If social control can be conceptualized as a quantitative variable, which exists in greater or lesser amounts in different settings,[40] then one way to summarize the argument of this chapter would be as follows: In a culture of weak ties, the quantity of social control will tend to be low.

5

The Moral Order of Strangers

Compared with large cities, suburbs have few public places where strangers intermingle. For this reason alone, conflict between unacquainted people in Hampton tends to be rare. In addition, predatory behavior by strangers—such as burglary and mugging—is quite infrequent. Even when individuals do encounter unknown offenders, they tend to avoid direct confrontation with them at all costs. The town's larger pattern of moral minimalism finds expression, where strangers are concerned, in an extreme aversion to any personal exercise of social control. Rather, townspeople leave the business of dealing with strangers almost exclusively to officials, most notably the police, and involve themselves very little in the maintenance of public order.

The Public Realm

Hampton's social organization prevents many conflicts between strangers from arising in the first place. This is so because it keeps unacquainted people away from one another to a degree not seen in cities, reducing the sorts of friction likely to arise in face-to-face encounters. As a primarily residential town, Hampton contains few public places which draw inhabitants from their private homes. There are a handful of restaurants and an even smaller number of bars, a few dozen retail shops, one library, one museum, one community pool, one live theater (in the summer), one movie theater, one bowling alley, one athletic club, and little else. Zoning laws cram the great majority of these together onto a strip of land running about four blocks along Main Street. The town's parks—mostly grassy, open spaces—are usually empty. It is this state of affairs, seen in suburb after suburb, which has earned for suburbia its reputation as a boring place.[1]

On their way to and from public locations, most people in the town ride in private automobiles. Indeed, comparatively few walk anywhere except to mail an occasional letter at a corner mailbox, to drop in on a near neighbor, or to exercise a dog; few make use of public transit. Partly because there are no destinations along most roads except private homes, and partly because residents drive when they have errands to do, there is very little street life in Hampton. It is possible to ride in a car for blocks at almost any time of day without encountering pedestrians. Even downtown, the streets are usually quiet.

Once citizens park their cars and emerge into public places, they still remain insulated from strangers to a degree not found in urban environments. For one thing, despite the fact that in this community of over 16,000 it is impossible for everyone to be acquainted with everyone else, people in public places are likely to meet someone they know. This is true along Main Street and even more so within establishments. Not only are those who pump their gas, cut their meat, or check out their library books frequently their acquaintances but so are other patrons and customers. In fact, many technically public places are actually used by the same people over and over again until all become acquaintances, or are commandeered by groups of friends for their own purposes. Thus, for instance, the commuter trains in and out of New York City are filled every day with men (and some women) who know one another by name, save seats for one another, share newspapers, and discuss world and local events. In the town's athletic club, many of those who jog on the track and sit in the sauna together have come to recognize each other and to carry on conversations about nonathletic matters. And at Hampton High School sporting events, which the same people attend throughout the school year, many spectators sit in the same seats time after time beside others who do likewise.

Unacquainted people, when they do meet on Hampton's streets or in shops, are in any case less unfamiliar to one another than urban strangers are. The social role of the stranger is partly defined by relational distance, the sheer absence of intimacy,[2] but also by cultural differences and marginalities of various sorts.[3] Because of the considerable homogeneity of the town's population, maintained with some effort by zoning at the formal level,[4] and apparently more informally by real-estate agents and banks, strangeness based on social and cultural differences is not widespread. Striking by their near absence are racial minorities and the very poor. As a result, the town's residents live for the most part in a world of their own.

Standards of Order

The relative isolation of people in Hampton from strangers is not only a fact of social morphology but also a moral expectation. It is one of the major yardsticks by which people measure order in public places on a daily basis and assess the conduct of strangers, so that those who disturb the town's protected world offend its inhabitants by doing so. Thus, for instance, individuals who use the streets or other public places more than is customary, especially for socializing, are seen as deviants. Young people are the greatest offenders in this regard, since they often congregate in public locations to smoke, snack, and talk. Other uses of the street may also arouse unfavorable notice. One young woman of about 18 years of age became known to many as "The Walker" and was seen as "mentally ill" because she was in the habit of strolling with her dog throughout town for hours on end. People responded similarly to an older woman who used to sit on a bench downtown for long periods of time and watch cars and pedestrians pass by.

Residents expect those they encounter in public places to go about their business not only expeditiously but also unobtrusively. Like people in other modern communities, they find grievances in a wide array of situational improprieties which they associate with mental disturbance or rowdiness. Individuals who approach others for no apparent reason, speak loudly to themselves or shout to companions, appear drunk on the streets, run recklessly among pedestrians, and engage in a variety of similar actions are met with disapproval.[5] It is expected that strangers will not impose themselves upon others and will proceed with caution and circumspection, both on foot and in cars.

Simply being in a public place at all can be offensive. Quiet residential streets, and the public parks scattered among them, are used on a day-by-day basis almost exclusively by neighborhood people. If outsiders appear in such locations, they are likely to arouse uneasiness or even alarm. Thus, one woman was disturbed and indignant to notice a man in a strange van sitting at the side of the road by her house. Other people have been singled out as "suspicious" while merely walking along residential streets. Even downtown, those who appear to be outsiders—by virtue of race or unconventionality—may effectively deviate by their very presence.

In many cases of this kind, the citizens of Hampton would explain their disapproval by voicing a fear of "crime"—by which they generally mean predatory behavior by strangers. Burglaries occur often enough to be a possibility for every household, but the chances of such victimization are slim. (During the period of this study there were about 100 burglaries per year—residential and commercial combined—recorded in police statistics, and contact with townspeople suggests that the great majority of such instances are reported.) It would appear that the most successful burglars are those who manage to blend in among the respectable citizens. For example, one pair responsible for several crimes were a middle-aged man and woman who dressed "well" and drove an expensive but "tasteful" car. Aside from burglaries, actions by strangers that would likely be handled as crimes—street muggings, assaults, and robberies, for instance—are virtually nonexistent. By town standards, the occasional exhibitionists who accost school children on the street are major criminals. Despite the low rate of predation, however, citizens are greatly concerned about crime and wary of people who seem out of place. They see strangers as potentially dangerous and anyone who is too conspicuous as alarming.[6]

One final way in which offenders may violate public order in Hampton should be mentioned here as well. Townspeople have standards of cleanliness and aesthetics to which they hold strangers as well as intimates. They are annoyed, for instance, by run-down houses and lots, and also by dirty shops and restaurants. It is difficult to say conclusively that standards of this sort are higher in Hampton than in less suburban places, but such appears to be the case. A single school bus, for example, parked in a municipal lot across from the town hall outraged many people as a visual blight that hurt the appearance of the community. In another instance, a minor furor erupted when one of the town's banks placed new name signs on the outside of its building. The signs were modernistic in design, made of plastic, and had the bank's logo printed in black, orange, and white. Many townspeople vehemently objected to what they claimed were garish and ugly signs, totally out of keeping with the more subdued character of Hampton's downtown areas. After numerous complaints poured into the bank's offices, town officials, and local newspapers, the bank voluntarily removed the signs. Hampton's residents would explain their concern about matters such as these partly as an effort to prevent their town from becoming what they consider nearby cities to be already—hopelessly disorganized and filthy places.

Strangers and Citizens

The citizens of Hampton are extremely reluctant to deal with offensive strangers personally. As much as they dislike hostile exchanges with family members or neighbors, they evidence even stronger aversion when unknown persons are involved. This is the most striking fact about the moral order prevailing among strangers in the town, and as a result, very little social control takes place between unacquainted people.

In fact, the immediate response of most individuals to a stranger's deviant action is to do nothing and wait for the offender to move on or for the situation to resolve itself. Sometimes, aggrieved people initiate avoidance by leaving the scene entirely. Even beyond single encounters, the responses of tolerance and avoidance are common. If the offender is someone likely to turn up again, or the offense of a sort likely to persist, people will often decide simply to absorb the deviance or to make efforts to prevent exposure to it in the future. In this way, several eccentric individuals whose behavior has been seen as abnormal have nonetheless escaped most sanctioning altogether. One was an older woman who, until her recent death, walked along the streets daily picking up all the litter she found, even the smallest specks of paper. As she did so, she muttered continually and unintelligibly under her breath. Another person, who recently moved out of town, commonly approached residents on the street and engaged them in meandering conversations which he refused to end. Yet another man frequented public places while drunk until, at some point, he gave up alcohol on his own initiative. In all of these cases, townspeople were remarkably tolerant of the unusual conduct involved, only commenting among themselves about it or seeking to avoid the offenders. They reacted in the same way to "The Walker" and to the woman who liked to sit for hours on a downtown bench. In addition, people similarly tolerate or avoid most "ugliness" or "filth" around the town, the case of the bank signs notwithstanding. They may comment disapprovingly about it to their family members or friends, but usually that is all they do.

Confrontation of any kind between strangers is so rare that this study uncovered only a handful of cases involving it, and just two that contained violence. In one of these intances, two youths in a car pulled into a driveway in front of a middle-aged jogger, who took offense and kicked the car's fender. When the young men got out of the car and found that it had been dented, they set off in pursuit of the jogger. Overtaking him, they demanded to know his name and that of his insurance company, and when he refused to answer them, they struck him with their fists. This case ended up in court, where it was the jogger who received the greater penalty and the sterner lecture. In the only other recorded matter in which violence occurred between strangers, a young man running through town collided with an older pedestrian, who thereupon punched him. When the victim of the blow summoned the police, the other man explained that he had thought he was being mugged. Incidents like these are strongly disapproved of by the public. So far as the townspeople are concerned, those who threaten or even criticize strangers are deviant for doing so. They are apt to be seen as "crazy" or "foolish" people who are "just asking for trouble."

The ease with which people can withdraw into their own private enclaves, leaving problems with strangers behind them, is a dimension of life in suburbia which its citizens appreciate greatly. In the language of animal ethology, it allows "flight" rather than "fight" when tensions arise between those who were previously unacquainted. However, the suburbanites of Hampton do not rely simply on tolerance or avoidance as ways of coping with strangers. Another favorite strategy for dealing with such individuals is to delegate to others the task of monitoring, approaching, and sanctioning them. Suburbanites thus like to leave their problems with strangers in the care of champions or surrogates, people who prosecute the grievances of others as if they were their own and, in so doing, "substitute for another person or group in the management of a conflict, largely or totally relieving a principal of responsibility and risk in the whole affair."[7] In Hampton, these champions are the police and administrative officials. As part of their job, they act upon complaints made by citizens against strangers, the overwhelming majority of which are anonymous or secret. Whereas calling the authorities about relatives or neighbors can mean an escalation in hostility, when strangers are concerned this is generally not the case because the offender never learns the identity of the complainant. For people who value nonconfrontation as much as suburbanites do, the use of champions only becomes appealing under the conditions of anonymity that prevail among strangers. Yet given this anonymity, it provides a way to get something done about grievances without requiring any personal exercise of social control at all. Even more desirable from the suburban point of view, these champions can prevent, uncover, and pursue much misconduct on their own, without even waiting for citizens to mobilize them.

In the view of Hampton's citizens, it is for their contribution in controlling strangers that they employ the police and administrative officers, and they measure the value of these officials by the extent to which they protect residents from unknown offenders. The precise techniques used toward this end are not of special interest, so long as they are effective and do not require citizen participation, since the town's residents do not want to be involved in any way.

Strangers and Champions

The role of champions in the social control of strangers has two dimensions in Hampton—preventive and remedial. Officials and townspeople seem to agree that the authorities should ideally prevent any misbehavior by strangers from occurring at all. Since the ideal is impossible in practice, however, officials are also responsible for confronting offensive strangers and restoring public order when it is violated. On a day-by-day basis, this means that officials spend their time in surveillance and in the discovery of wrongdoing as well as in initiating encounters with offenders and responding to citizen complaints about them. In practice, the preventive function consumes the greater part of the time these champions spend on the job; the isolation of unknown people from one another and the high rates of tolerance and avoidance in the town reduce the number of citizen complaints that command attention. Overall, the police carry most of the burden of regulating strangers, although administrative officers from the Zoning Office and the Board of Health assist in part of the work.

The Police

When municipal police forces first appeared in England and the United States, their explicit mandate was to maintain public order in the face of increasingly diverse and unstable urban populations.[8] How they have fared in this endeavor is a controversial question. It seems clear, however, that the sorts of problems the early police were asked to solve—such as predation by strangers, interpersonal violence, and rioting by mobs—were then and still are much more prevalent in cities than in suburbs.[9] Nonetheless, the citizens of Hampton view police as essential to their peace and well-being, and credit them with tremendous preventive impact upon "crime." As long as the police stay out of their intimate relations with their peers, the townspeople are very supportive of them. In this, they are apparently like suburbanites elsewhere.[10]

Hampton maintains a police force of just over 30 officers, internally specialized and stratified. There is both a small detective and traffic division, and a chief, a deputy chief, a captain, 2 lieutenants, 7 sergeants, about 5 detectives, and about 15 patrol officers. At the time of this study, all officers were white males. According to the police chief diligent efforts to locate qualified women and blacks had not succeeded. One woman in whom the department had expressed an interest failed a psychiatric screening when it was found that she had "violent propensities." (Since this study, two black officers and one woman were hired, but the woman has already resigned to escape alleged harassment by her male colleagues.)

In carrying out their mission to maintain public order, officers in Hampton, as in many other suburbs, largely adopt what has been called a "service style" of policing. They maintain a visible presence in the community, respond to the great majority of calls for assistance which they receive, intervene often on their own initiative where they have public support to do so, and work cooperatively with the town's residents.[11] In practice, they concentrate their efforts on three specific areas of concern: the conduct of young people, the movements of suspicious persons, and traffic violations. These are both the things about which the police initiate the most activity on their own and also the ones citizens are most likely to complain about. It should be noted that none of the main targets of police action in Hampton involves wrongdoing of a sort likely to cause concern in nearby cities. Rather, it seems that the virtual absence of predation and violence in the town has left the police and the townspeople free to direct their energies elsewhere. The result is that much more attention is paid to things that would seem trivial in urban centers. This pattern is consistent with the classic hypothesis that people will always find something in the behavior of others against which to exercise social control— whatever the objective conduct might be:

> Imagine a society of saints, a perfect cloister of exemplary individuals. Crimes, properly so called, will there be unknown; but faults which

appear venial to the layman will create there the same scandal that the ordinary offense does in ordinary circumstances.[12]

Applied to the work of officials, this hypothesis claims that, even where all conventional crime has been contained, "it is still improbable that the existing control machinery would go unused. More likely, the agencies of control would turn their attention to other forms of behavior."[13] This seems exactly what has happened in Hampton. The town's citizens, watching from the sidelines, urge their champions on as they cope with the most pressing problems of public disorder this typical suburb contains.

YOUTHFUL DISORDER

In Hampton, as in American society more generally, young people are continually found to violate the normative standards which define public order. (For these purposes, the category of "young people" includes both juveniles and legal adults in their early twenties.) The absence of a depressed minority of poor or homeless people, who rival or exceed adolescents as a focus of police attention in urban areas, renders young people especially prominent in the suburbs. Some commentators have even remarked that youths take the place of an underclass in suburban communities.[14] In any event, it is clear that the police and public in Hampton regard juveniles and young adults as a disorderly and bothersome class of people.

Much of the trouble with young people in the town seems to be that they socialize in groups in public places and engage in unconventional and boisterous expressive behavior. Both of these patterns arise ultimately from a distinctive youth subculture forged mostly in the town's schools. Thrown into one another's company in large numbers for long periods of time, greatly outnumbering the adults who supervise them, students develop strong ties among themselves and modes of behavior all their own. When they leave school, they carry these with them. In this sense, education is a major cause of the perceived problem young people represent in Hampton.

Improper use of the streets and other public places attracts much police notice. The demand by young people for a place to congregate away from adults is so strong, however, that all the police can do in this regard may best be spoken of as containment. Theirs is a constant effort to keep within bounds what they have found to be an intractable problem. Thus, they will arrest or, more often, simply disperse young people who attempt to move into parts of town previously undisturbed by them, while allowing them some freedom to associate in other areas. When a young man and his girlfriend were discovered on the roof of the library at four in the morning, they were arrested on the spot. This was clearly off limits. Downtown, the police keep knots of young people off the main streets, although they allow some to stand and talk a block or so away.

Occasionally misunderstandings emerge among the police, young people, and adult citizens about how much disorder will be tolerated in given places. One such matter attracted a great deal of attention:

> Patrolman Rossi was a new member of the Hampton Police Department when he encountered about a dozen black youths standing on a street corner a block from downtown. (The youths were part of the town's small black population.) Finding them disorderly, he told the group to disperse and go home. They protested that they had always done what they were doing without interference in the past and insisted that another officer be summoned to the scene to explain matters to the new policeman. The incident was defused when a seasoned officer arrived and managed with some difficulty to define the situation as one in which the young people had been unusually loud and boisterous. This tacitly affirmed their right to gather on the street corner when they were more quiet. The episode created hard feelings which contributed a few months later to the only "riot" in town memory. On this occasion the same young people were socializing in public again, this time in a parking lot near the location of the earlier encounter. Allegedly in response to calls from irate neighbors bothered by noise, the police arrived and ordered them to go home. Again they resisted, and this time fighting broke out with both sides calling for reinforcements. The police cars parked at the scene had their windows smashed; people on both sides sustained minor injuries. The police chief was called to help restore order, and it was a few hours before the youths dispersed. In the following days, the police

arrested three black "ringleaders." Community sentiment was mixed, with many people sympathetic to the boys. Even one newly retired police officer remarked that the whole incident was "a shame" that would never have happened if the police officers who had gone to the scene initially had had any "common sense." Ultimately, the three accused youths were each sentenced after appeal to a $500 fine and 45 days in jail, and the police department hired its first black officer within a few months.

It more often happens, however, that adult citizens support the police wholeheartedly in their efforts against juveniles who assemble in public places, if anything finding them too lax or too lenient. In fact, a notably large proportion of complaints citizens make to the police are about groups of "disorderly" young people who have escaped official intervention. One of the most serious breaches of the peace—as measured by citizen reaction—involved such a matter:

On a warm spring evening, students at a private high school in Hampton hosted an officially sanctioned dance on their campus. As usual during such affairs, off-duty members of the Hampton Police Department were on hand to help keep the peace. As the teenagers left the dance and the scrutiny of the officers, however, many chose not to go home directly but rather to prolong the evening. A few dozen wandered off through the neighborhood surrounding the high school, working their way slowly downtown. They drank, smoked, played portable radios, and conversed as they moved along the streets, and in the quiet otherwise prevailing around midnight, they created a commotion. Occasionally two or three would break away from the larger groups and slip onto someone's private property, sitting down under trees or along bushes. Many also dropped empty beer and soda cans or cigarette packs at curbs and on lawns. All of this offended dozens of residents along their route. Apparently no one came or shouted outside to confront the young people directly, but numerous phone calls were made to the police. Officers promptly responded and dispersed the teenagers wherever they came upon them, but when the offended homeowners noticed their trampled and littered lawns the following morning, another round of phone calls began. These were to criticize the police for allowing such a problem to arise in the first place and for not resolving it more quickly when it did happen. The mayor, town council members, and school officials also received complaints about the incident. In the end, new guidelines for high school social functions were created; most notable among them was a provision for increasing the number of off-duty police and other responsible adults available to serve as sentries for surrounding streets.

Another, more chronic problem of public disorder that caused much citizen concern also involved young people:

> In Hampton, there is no designated place outside the home where young people can gather away from adult supervision. There is, however, apparently a tremendous demand for such a place. One summer, teenagers began to use the grounds surrounding a local ice-cream parlor for this purpose. The "invasion" began slowly and increased through the months. As evening fell, dozens of teenagers would converge upon the store, buy ice-cream cones or sundaes, and then sit outside for hours talking on the steps, the hoods of cars, the sidewalks, and the lawn of the Elks Club across the street. Older people found this very offensive, and many responded by simply avoiding the place. Others called the police to complain. Citizens refrained, however, from criticizing the young people personally, preferring instead (if in their presence at all) to scurry past them as quickly as possible, eyes averted. Eventually the police succeeded, with the support of the store's manager, in discouraging the young people from assembling at the ice-cream parlor by dispersing them repeatedly. No sooner was the problem resolved there, however, than the young people began to gather at a fast-food hamburger outlet down the street. Calls to the police resumed. A few months later, the hamburger store was quiet, and the young people had moved on to a donut shop nearby.

Young people also attract a great deal of police attention for things other than socializing in public places. One officer arrested a young man for throwing a Frisbee across Main Street. Another arrested a youth for pulling a traffic cone into a moving car in which he was a passenger. Young people have found themselves in police custody for starting fires in piles of leaves, throwing beer bottles out of car windows, and for setting off firecrackers. In addition to disorderly conduct such as this and the drinking of alcoholic beverages which often accompanies it, vandalism is a major occasion for police sanctioning of juveniles. In two extreme incidents, one at a golf course and the other in Hampton High School, young people caused thousands of dollars worth of property damage in a single evening. More often, they break a few windows or write a few words on the sides of buildings. Young people have been known to uproot plants designed to beautify public places, to scratch, paint over, or remove traffic signs, and to shoot at traffic lights with BB guns or slingshots. One young man was arrested for a felony called "possession of a concealed deadly weapon"—in this case a slingshot—because the police were certain that he had been using it to break car windows in parking lots. (The officers were upset when the county prosecutor sent the case back to the municipal level for trial as a misdemeanor on the grounds that a slingshot is not a deadly weapon.)

In their encounters with young people, the police generally do no more than question, warn, or issue orders to disperse. They do, however, take about 500 juveniles per year into custody. (This accounts for about 60 percent of offenders in all nontraffic cases "solved" by the police.) Official statistics indicate that about 15 to 20 percent of juveniles who are formally charged with offenses are sent to the county juvenile court, while the great majority receive some more informal disposition.[15] In Hampton, about half of those who are not turned over to county authorities are simply released into the custody of their parents. The other half are referred to two local agencies of social control, the Juvenile Conference Committee and a counseling program run by therapists under police auspices. The Juvenile Conference Committee consists of several adult citizens who meet every month or so to consider the offenses of young people. In comparatively nonaccusatory proceedings, they meet with the offenders and their parents to "discuss" the youths' behavior. Even so, they usually impose community-work sentences on the young people, such as mowing lawns in public areas, cleaning the sides of buildings presumably marked by other juveniles, and painting town benches. Occasionally youths are sentenced to do research, as when an offender found with marijuana was asked to write a documented paper outlining the negative effects of the drug on the human body. The chairwoman of this committee reports some trouble with middle-class parents who resent having their children assigned to manual labor, but finds people generally cooperative. The relatively new counseling program is run by three citizens with a social-work background and is designed to provide counseling for "troubled" juveniles and their families. Once young people become legal adults, they are liable to prosecution in the municipal and county courts. About a fourth of all nontraffic matters raised in the municipal court involve charges brought by the police against young adults for disorderly conduct, drug use, and similar offenses.

As a group, young people in Hampton seem to harbor a great deal of resentment against the police. The police, for their part, mirror community sentiment in finding young people a major social problem and persistent source of disorder. This is so even though young people in the town are peaceful by the standards of urban places, where juveniles and young adults are much more often involved in violent and predatory crime. In Hampton, if something disorderly strikes adult eyes—a traffic sign twisted or broken off its post, for instance, or a piece of litter left in a public area—the immediate response of most adults is that "the kids must have done it." (This is true in numerous cases where the damage might well have been caused by natural forces such as wind and weather.) In many places around the world, people believe in unseen creatures—like leprechauns, imps, and djinns— who delight in causing mischief and inconveniencing humans. In Hampton, young people take the place of these mythical trouble-makers. Adult citizens, who are unwilling to step forward them-selves to deal with the perceived problem, depend on the police for a solution.

SUSPICIOUS PERSONS

Another major focus of police concern in suburbia is the discovery and control of "suspicious persons." In light of what has already been said, it should not be surprising that many suspicious people are young adults. In general, however, this problem is distinct from that represented by unruly youths. Suspicious persons tend to be older, are usually unknown to the police, and are generally found alone or with one or two companions. What distinguishes them from others is that they are out of place—in locations where strangers of any kind are uncommon or where people with their particular social characteristics are rarely seen.

The movements of suspicious persons, like the behavior of young people, seem to arouse more concern in the town than they would in nearby cities, where other matters appear more pressing. Police encounters with suspicious persons arise both from citizen complaints and from police surveillance. Town residents share with the police a belief that people who are out of place are potentially dangerous, and also a firm conviction that ordinary citizens should never approach such individuals themselves but should leave that job to the authorities. Thus, in one case, a woman who noticed a stranger parked in a van along her roadside called the police to deal with him rather than confront him personally. Another citizen telephoned to report that "strange people" were walking through an old estate across the street. A third called to say that a stranger in a car had slowed down alongside her children when they were walking home from school and had then driven off. She gave a description of the man and hoped the police could locate him and question him. In a fourth case, an elderly woman called the police because she heard a man's voice outside her home one evening. Someone else called to report a "prowler" at the home of a vacationing neighbor.

The extent to which people depend on the police to be their champions in confrontations with suspicious persons can be documented through information provided by the police department. Overall, Hampton's police force, staffed by slightly more than 30 officers, receives about 30 calls from citizens per day, or about 1,000 per month. Among these are frequent requests for nonlegal assistance of various kinds (about a third of the total) and calls seeking information from the police or imparting information to them about matters other than offenses—such as when citizens will be out of town (about 10 to 15 percent of the total). Another third allege actual offenses of some kind, while the remainder—accounting for nearly a fourth of all calls—report suspicious persons or circumstances. (The latter might be, for example, an open window in a vacationing neighbor's house.) Domestic disputes and public disturbances together account for less than 3 percent of all calls. By way of comparison, on a single day in 1964 the Chicago police received about 5,000 calls.[16] The overall rate of calls was thus similar to that in Hampton (just under two calls daily per 1,000 people in each place). The substance of the calls was quite different, however, with the citizens of Chicago asking their police to intervene much more frequently in actual confrontations. One-quarter of the calls in Chicago were made about ongoing fights. Fewer callers asked the Chicago police for nonlegal assistance or imparted information about matters other than crimes, and only 4 percent reported suspicious persons.

The physical organization of Hampton—which allows residents to monitor their neighborhoods and to spot outsiders who linger in their areas—in itself may account for the comparatively large number of calls about suspicious persons. In a large city such as Chicago or New York with high population densities and a steady flow of diverse people, it is more difficult to single out a few among the many strangers to label as especially suspicious.[17] At the same time, Hampton's less-burdened police welcome calls reporting suspicious persons and circumstances in a way that inner-city police might not. They even actively solicit such business from citizens in conversations and through articles written periodically by the police chief for the local newspaper.

The police also uncover many suspicious persons on their own. Given the near absence of assaults, muggings, and other events that would take priority in the allocation of police service, officers in Hampton have a great deal of time to search for those who strike them as potential criminals. The kinds of persons they are watching for virtually never materialize, however. Thus, one fear of many townspeople is that poor blacks or Hispanics from New York or other nearby cities will enter the town and prey upon its residents. A couple of well-publicized incidents in which this occurred have helped to convince many that such predation is a serious threat. A person who appeared to be from an urban ghetto would surely arouse police concern and would quite likely be approached. On a day-by-day basis, however, such people are essentially never seen in Hampton. They have little occasion to be there, and they are probably well aware of how cold their welcome would be. Nonetheless, suspicious persons of other sorts do turn up in the town:

A police officer on routine patrol was driving through a parking lot one night when he noticed a person he found to be suspicious emerging from a downtown building. This was a man of about thirty, dressed in worn blue jeans and a leather jacket. The officer, though he patrolled the area regularly, did not recognize him. He approached the man and asked if he were looking for someone. The man answered "yes," that he had come to visit a friend who lived in one of the upstairs apartments (located over a retail store), but the friend was not at home. The officer asked for the friend's name, and the man told him. After watching the man walk off, the officer entered the building and went upstairs to make sure that everything was in order.

A suspicious person was discovered one night sleeping in a parking lot in a car with out-of-state license plates. He was a man in his twenties or thirties, dressed in old, rumpled clothes and wearing a leather jacket. The officer who came upon him rapped on the window of the car with his nightstick, startling the man inside who woke up and proceeded to drive down the street. The officer then walked back to his own car and set off after the suspicious man. A few blocks away, he found him—pulled over to the side of the road and preparing to go back to sleep. This time when the policeman approached him, the man rolled down his window and carried on a conversation. The officer smelled liquor on his breath and promptly arrested him for drunken driving. It subsequently turned out that the man was a soldier stationed in the South who had come to Hampton to visit his daughter and ex-wife. While there, he had stopped in a bar and had become drunk, after which he had decided to sleep for a while in his car before attempting to drive.

Generally, the police do not arrest suspicious persons, but rather simply interrogate them and allow them to go on their way. Sometimes, officers write up "contact reports" based on their encounters with suspicious persons and file these in the station. It may well be that the police use the process of writing a contact report to intimidate those whom they find suspicious. This would be consistent with their larger strategy for dealing with such people—letting them know that the town's guardians have detected them and are watching their every move.

TRAFFIC

Traffic enforcement is another major part of the work of the Hampton police. In an average month, they issue nearly 200 citations for moving violations and another 400 or so for parking offenses; in addition, they give numerous informal warnings and lectures. The department is equipped with the latest radar technology, and officers frequently use it, lying in wait by the side of the road for drivers who ignore the posted speed limits. While they are on ordinary patrol duty too, the police watch for bad drivers as well as for suspicious persons.

The concern with traffic enforcement seems to have many social roots. One is simply the high standard of orderliness which prevails in the town, and which extends to the flow of automobiles as well as to the movement of pedestrians and the upkeep of public areas. Another is the amount of free time which the police have available in order to monitor traffic. In the relative absence of violence and stranger predation, the offenses of drivers seem worse and can be more actively pursued. In this sense, bad driving is another kind of "deviance among saints" in the suburbs. (Supporting evidence that driving violations loom larger where predatory crime is infrequent comes from a recent study which found that the relationship between traffic tickets issued by the police and robbery rates is inverse.[18]) At the same time, careful monitoring of the flow of traffic provides a means for the police to scrutinize the comings and goings of outsiders and thus to extend their persistent search for suspicious persons. Citizens and police alike view the roads—especially Main Street, part of a larger state highway which links many small towns to the expressways serving New York—as the route by which threatening outsiders could find their way to town. Largely for this reason, public resistance to a state proposal for the modernization and extension of Main Street has been high in Hampton and surrounding communities, and the plan has been considerably delayed. People would rather bear the inconvenience of narrow and congested streets on a day-by-day basis than make it easier for the inhabitants of New York City to reach the town. Since they cannot do away with streets altogether, however, they turn to the police to scrutinize those who use them. Finally, traffic laws provide the police with a weapon they find valuable in the control of young and unconventional persons.

It seems clear that the sorts of traffic offenses which attract police attention in Hampton would often escape notice elsewhere. Thus, the police take seriously the 25 mile-per-hour speed limits along most roads which the residents of Hampton's neighborhoods have successfully defended for years. Radar traps are often set up at the bottom of hills on such roads, and violators are commonly caught there. (In fact, the only way to obey the speed limit in many of these places is to ride one's brakes continually for long stretches at a time.) Another routine activity of the police is to station an officer in hiding at any of various intersections throughout the town in order to discover drivers rolling through stop signs. A third offense which concerns officers is what they term "passing on the right." Their understanding of the relevant law is that it prohibits drivers from pulling alongside other cars at red traffic lights and then proceeding around them when the light turns green. Many drivers apparently interpret this law differently. The police in Hampton also have a much stricter interpretation of what it means to "proceed through a red light" than many drivers do. People who choose to keep moving through amber lights or who anticipate the change of a red light to green may run afoul of an officer. Even the definition of an accident is unusually strict in Hampton, encompassing incidents involving a single automobile and minor damage. People proceeding on their way after such events have been arrested for "leaving the scene of an accident"—a serious charge. A last example can be seen in the enforcement of a municipal ordinance prohibiting on-the-street parking between 2:00 and 6:00 A.M. Promptly at 2:00 each morning, the police begin a systematic canvassing of every street in the town, looking for violators.

Official statistics do not mirror the full extent of traffic enforcement, since informal dispositions of offenders are common. Despite the fact that tickets can often be settled by mail, traffic offenses account for most of the business of the town's municipal court. They are taken very seriously there by everyone concerned. All receive full hearings from the judge, who sometimes resolves them by going personally to the scene of alleged violations. Defendants commonly appear with attorneys (about one-fourth of the time), witnesses, or even with charts and diagrams. One man revealed that he had spent hours preparing for his trial on the charge of failing to come to a complete stop at a stop sign by researching the matter in a law library. When traffic cases are contested, the prosecutor routinely participates, accounting for nearly all of the times in which he does take an advocate's role in the courtroom. In general, young people in their teens and twenties account for the great majority of the traffic defendants in court, although it is older defendants who more often contest the charges against them.

The concern with traffic enforcement in Hampton appears to have a considerable impact on the tenor of day-to-day life in the town. The fact that the police are so aggressive about traffic invests them with an aura of aggressiveness in general. People feel that the authorities are strict, and that they will not tolerate breaches of the public order. In this way, traffic enforcement has an effect which resonates into many areas of social life.[19]

Just as they do where youthful disorder and suspicious persons are concerned, citizens generate a great deal of police business in regard to traffic problems. They do so by reporting automobile accidents. There are an average of 45 such cases each month, the great majority of which involve two drivers.[20] In keeping with their aversion to confrontation of any kind, especially where strangers are concerned, townspeople involved in accidents virtually never have altercations with each other. They simply call the police, exchange names and insurance information, and go their separate ways. They seem to invest little emotionally in their driving, take no particular pride in it, and do not experience it as a challenge to honor to be implicated in an accident. For them, automobile accidents are largely misfortunes akin to fires and floods.

In the aftermath of an accident, the police are called upon to see that the injured receive medical attention and that the drivers exchange all necessary information about their insurance coverage. Sometimes officers issue traffic citations to drivers they consider to be greatly in the wrong, but the police are not ultimately responsible for a resolution in traffic accidents. That job falls to insurance companies. Indeed, if conflicts can be conceptualized as property,[21] then automobile accidents in Hampton actually belong to these companies and not to the drivers who create them. To some degree, this has long been true in the town, where the comfortable incomes of citizens have made insurance a readily affordable commodity. It has become especially true recently, however, since the passage of a so-called no-fault law which is binding throughout the state in which Hampton is located. When an accident happens, the new law has established that each driver's insurance company will assume his or her expenses without regard to who was responsible for the collision. (At a later time, the companies may then negotiate between themselves about which should bear the costs of the accident.) The new law also makes insurance coverage mandatory.

Turning automobile accidents over to insurance companies transforms potential interpersonal conflict into little more than a matter of paperwork, something to be processed routinely and without emotion. Knowing that an insurance company will compensate them for their losses makes it easier for the two drivers to treat each other with civility at the accident scene; this is understandable, since they are not then really adversaries. It is consistent with their management of conflict more generally that suburbanites are very pleased with such a way of handling automobile accidents and would like to see it extended to a variety of problems now processed in a more confrontative fashion, such as accidents of other kinds and consumer complaints.[22] They find it much more "civilized" to resolve claims without contention and ill will. What is more, they are reasonably comfortable and confident in dealing with insurance companies. They would much rather work out their problems with calm professionals in offices than with ordinary strangers placed in their paths by bad luck.

Administrative Officers

Although the police bear most of the burden of regulating strangers in Hampton, substituting for a citizenry unwilling to perform the task, they do receive some assistance from the town's administrative officers. These people—zoning officers and sanitarians—perform primarily aesthetic and hygienic functions, working to preserve beauty and cleanliness in the community. Both act on occasional complaints from citizens and also pursue matters on their own initiative. The targets of their attention include such wrongdoers as the managers of shops and restaurants not deemed clean enough, individuals who leave disabled cars in their driveways or other visible locations, and the owners of unkempt lots who purportedly have violated ordinances against rodent harborage or weed overgrowth. One of the biggest cases in the Zoning Office involved a horse:

> Mr. Zack was a middle-aged man of considerable means and prominence in the local business community who lived in a large home with expansive grounds. On his property when he purchased it was an old barn once used to stable horses. After owning the place for some time, Mr. Zack bought a horse and housed it in the barn. It happens, however, that horses are restricted in Hampton, and when a local police officer observed the animal while on routine patrol, he promptly notified the Zoning Office. Approached and told to sell the horse or make arrangements for its housing elsewhere, Mr. Zack balked. He argued that since the barn had been on his property before he purchased it, maintaining a horse was an established preexistent use of the land and therefore he was exempt from the prohibition of the ordinance. The zoning officers countered that there had not been a horse in the barn for so long that the use had been abandoned and had not in fact existed for years. Mr. Zack continued to resist and appealed the issue to the full Zoning Board. A hearing was finally held and Mr. Zack—backed by his neighbors—succeeded in carrying his point. The zoning officers were very disgruntled and felt that the offender, because of his high status, had received special leniency.

Unlike the police, the administrative officers have a low profile in the town, and many citizens are barely aware of their existence. The zoning officers and sanitarians consider this a proper state of affairs. The more efficiently they perform their duties, keeping Hampton clean and beautiful, the less problematic their function should be and the less visible their role. At the same time, they and all who are acquainted with their work feel strongly that it is important to have officials to maintain sanitation and aesthetic standards in the town. Ordinary citizens are considered unable to identify and to pursue violators. Most convinced of this are the citizens themselves, who generally want no part in regulating the public in any way and who are more than happy to delegate the job.

Finally, it should be noted that the town's governing officials—the mayor and council members—also play a role in the control of strangers. Although they are not charged with the day-to-day preservation of public order, they are responsible for seeing that local ordinances are enforced. In performing this function, they sometimes pressure the police and administrative officers to engage in more vigorous prosecution of offenders. This may be in response to citizen complaints or may arise from their own concern. Their work in this regard establishes elected officials as important guardians of peacefulness and cleanliness throughout the community and as another group of people who serve as champions for a citizenry unwilling to deal with troublesome strangers on their own.

Strangers and Moral Minimalism

This chapter has described the extreme aversion of Hampton's suburbanites to open confrontation with strangers, or indeed to the exercise of any kind of direct social control against them. So thoroughgoing is this sentiment of aversion to open confrontation that the business of regulating strangers and maintaining public order is largely delegated to officials. Citizens view these officials as absolutely essential and support them financially with few questions asked. Should an offender manage to elude them—and to be encountered within the greatly limited range of public life—citizens will usually tolerate or avoid that person, or they may invoke an official in secret. After automobile accidents, they withdraw calmly to file claims with insurance companies.

The sheer insulation from strangers that prevails in suburbia, the rarity of predation by outsiders, and the efficiency and helpfulness of officials all help to make this strategy of disengagement feasible and attractive. There appear to be other dynamics at work, however. Since the comparatively weak and restrained nature of social control between relatives and neighbors in Hampton is largely the result of the atomization, transiency, and autonomy of the town's population, and since it is among strangers that these attributes are most prominent, it is not surprising that there social control is least forcefully exerted by the citizens themselves.

Weak ties and social dispersion among strangers undermine direct and forceful responses to grievances in some of the same ways that they do in other relationships. Partly, they make offenses by strangers less persistent and less bothersome. Thus, the brief duration of meetings between unacquainted persons helps to make the costs of tolerance low, since problems that arise will usually be temporary. Furthermore, since strangers who come together casually in public places know nothing about one another's past histories and reputations, they cannot detect chronic or repeat offenders and react accordingly. In most instances, avoidance or retreat will be readily possible should a stranger prove so annoying that mere tolerance is not an adequate solution. At the same time, atomization and autonomy among strangers also directly reduces the willingness or ability to be forceful. People's many responsibilities or activities in other settings command their attention, leaving them little time or energy to invest in grievances against strangers. At the same time, the mutual independence of people who encounter each other by chance in public places reduces the range of possible sanctions available to them. Violence, though theoretically feasible, is unattractive to isolated people without support groups at hand. Secret recourse to officials is effectively the only option that allows people to do more than simply tolerate or avoid offenders without also requiring a confrontation. What is crucial about this response is that the anonymity prevailing among strangers virtually guarantees that the objects of any complaints will never know who has invoked the authorities against them. Or better yet from the suburban point of view, in many cases officials will discover offensive conduct on their own and move to control it, relieving citizens even of the need to voice their grievances.

Since transiency and atomization are properties of social life between strangers throughout modern societies, and should everywhere have similar effects, it is understandable that moral interaction in public places seems generally minimal and restrained. Many observers have commented on the extremes of tolerance and avoidance seen among strangers in urban America and upon the rarity of open confrontation—even criticism—among them. First of all, people appear to time their movements in public places so as to avoid altogether individuals or situations likely to be annoying or to arouse conflict.[23] Once face to face, strangers seem to have adapted to one another's presence with what one social scientist has described as an ethos of noninvolvement and nonconcern, partly because as isolated individuals each is highly vulnerable to every other.[24] Another researcher has documented the use of studied inattention (something which in practice entails a great deal of tolerance) and flight from unpleasant situations as techniques for the management of offensive or threatening conduct by strangers in urban areas.[25] In a study of social interaction and social control on a crowded beach outside Los Angeles, an investigation has found that tolerance, avoidance, and the delegation of order maintenance to authorities (the police and lifeguards) are the three major means used to prevent and resolve "trouble." The peaceful and pleasant nature of activities on the beach results precisely because people there are isolated from one another and encapsulated in their private worlds.[26]

Yet as weakly as people in the industrialized West are tied to strangers, and as little as they exert moral sanctions against them, to the suburbanites of Hampton it is still too much. If these people were to have their way, ties to strangers would be even weaker. Simply having to deal with socially distant persons—however civil the interchanges—makes them uncomfortable. Correcting the behavior of strangers is much worse. Thus, in the best of all possible worlds, they would exercise no moral authority against strangers whatsoever.

6

Conclusion

Moral minimalism dominates the suburbs. On a day-by-day basis, life is filled with efforts to deny, minimize, contain, and avoid conflict. People shun confrontations and show great distaste for the pursuit of grievances or the censure of wrongdoing. In fact, only when they can be assured that someone else will bear the full burden of moral authority, allowing them to remain completely anonymous and uninvolved, do suburbanites approve the exercise of social control. This syndrome of conflict aversion and moral restraint has as hallmarks a great deal of tolerance and frequent resort to avoidance when tensions arise.

The pervasive moral minimalism found in the suburbs contrasts sharply with claims that American society is particularly violent or litigious.[1] However true such characterizations may be for other settings, they do not reflect suburban reality. Residents of suburbs like Hampton rarely aggress against one another physically, and for them, law remains primarily a theoretical option for handling grievances that arise in their everyday lives. They are happy to have police act as their champions in preventing and resolving trouble that unknown persons might cause, but beyond this, they have very little use for law. When problems occur, most people do not seriously consider recourse to legal officials, and, in fact, they generally act as if law did not exist at all. In this sense, suburbia is a kind of limited anarchy. The evidence from the suburbs suggests, then, that the penetration of law into American life has been considerably more limited in its range and effect than is commonly believed. Furthermore, this accords with what has recently been learned about Americans in other settings who similarly use law far less often than they would be entitled to do so, including the Southerners described by Greenhouse, the urban Northeasterners described by Thomas-Buckle and Buckle, the rural Midwesterners described by Engel, and the Western cattle ranchers described by Ellickson.[2] The behavior of people in the suburbs thus lends support to recent reevaluations that have taken issue with the portrayal of a contentious and litigious American population struggling to gain access to already overburdened courts.[3]

More generally, moral minimalism as it appears in American suburbs is a most unusual phenomenon in cross-cultural perspective. Avoidance, which is one of its most prominent features, seems to have been common among hunting and gathering peoples but to have been greatly overshadowed in virtually all more developed societies by various forms of moralistic confrontation, whether involving law, mediation, negotiation, or violence such as feuding and fighting. Few other groups have ever left so simultaneously undeveloped both the means for aggressive retaliation and those for the nonviolent airing and resolution of disputes, whether legally or otherwise.

The patterns of social stratification and social morphology found in suburbia, themselves distinctive cross-culturally, can account for this unusual moral order. People in the suburbs move in and out of relationships frequently and live their lives under conditions of privacy, individuation, material independence, and freedom from authority, all the while surrounded by a wide variety of competing interests and associates. This makes avoidance of moral trouble feasible and attractive, and confrontation less so. It shortens the lifespan of conflicts, for example, provides ready avenues of escape from offenders, distracts people from the annoyances they encounter, retards the accumulation of grudges and the growth of enmities, deprives people of allies, and undermines intervention by third parties. As a result, moral minimalism flourishes.

Support for these claims comes partly from differences in behavior readily observable in the town selected for this study. There, in comparison to middle-class residents, the working-class people are less migratory and tend to be embedded in more intimate and interconnected social networks. When grievances arise, these people are more likely to confront offenders violently or to seek the intervention of officials, who are generally of higher status than themselves. Young people, whose day-to-day lives are less fragmented than those of their elders, are also more inclined to confront their antagonists. Since working-class residents and young people have much in common with middle-class adults, however, they too exhibit a great deal of moral minimalism.

The analysis presented here suggests that moral minimalism, with its aversion to conflict and its preference for restraint, will be found wherever social life approximates the suburban model. The necessary factors include independence among people, arising from equality, autonomy, and self-sufficiency; individuation, in which people act on their own without group support; social fragmentation, in which each person's involvements and associates are widely scattered and unique; and social fluidity, in which people are highly mobile, both physically and interpersonally, and move in and out of relationships constantly. On the other hand, the analysis suggests that more socially cohesive, interdependent, interconnected, and stratified settings will be inimical to moral minimalism. In such places, either aggression or some form of settlement should dominate the moral order.

These claims are meant to apply to the ways in which people actually behave in the face of grievances, rather than to their attitudes and opinions. There is, nonetheless, an ethical philosophy associated with moral minimalism, one which both expresses and sustains it. There is also a distinctive understanding of people's positive obligations that seems to accompany moral minimalism and to arise from the same sources. Both of these features of a morally minimalistic environment are of interest in their own right.

The Philosophy of Moral Minimalism

There is a system of ethical beliefs that goes hand in hand with moral minimalism in the suburbs and that specifies proper procedure in the righting of wrongs. Consideration of this philosophy is not only relevant to an understanding of the moral order of suburbia, but may also reveal the ethical superstructure of moral restraint in general. In Hampton, the most basic component of this system is a strong conviction that conflict is a social contaminant, something to be prevented if at all possible and to be ended quickly once begun. Should interpersonal conflict have positive functions or be in any sense a desirable property of social life,[4] these suburbanites are unaware of it.

This orientation expresses itself in various ways. For one thing, it is associated with a considerable degree of embarrassment and discomfort evident in the town's residents whenever interpersonal tensions arise and with an eagerness to conceal these tensions from others. Like sex and income, if not more so, conflict is a sensitive subject in Hampton. One of the town's police officers remarked that the incidents recorded in the police logs were "touchy matters" requiring the utmost in confidentiality. This is exactly the view held by the townspeople.

Related to the negative assessment of conflict is the attitude that the exercise of social control is dirty and unpleasant work. This extends not only to aggressive tactics such as violence—which is felt to be extremely distasteful—but also to many efforts simply to reach a peaceful accommodation with an offender. Even when it comes to nothing more than making a casual request of a neighbor to change some bothersome practice, people in the town must generally overcome a considerable reluctance. In the debate between husbands and wives about who will perform such missions, there is often no resolution, and as a result, many offenders are effectively pardoned altogether. This attitude also generates considerable sympathy for people, like police officers and judges, who must routinely exercise social control as part of their jobs. From the point of view of cultures which prosecute grievances more forcefully, suburbanites might well appear cowardly.

For their part, people in suburbs like Hampton have very negative opinions about those who opt for confrontation in the face of interpersonal tension. An individual who is quick to take offense is likely to become the butt of private ridicule at the very least. Someone prone to the exercise of violence is likely to be labeled "mentally ill"; the causes of "a problem" of this kind are often theorized to lie in childhood experiences or possible use of illicit drugs. People generally avoid those viewed as contentious, not simply to express disapproval but also to prevent becoming the focus of their objectionable and unreasonable conduct in the future.

The dislike of confrontation contrasts sharply with the strongly positive opinion of tolerance and avoidance held by people in Hampton. Simply staying away from someone who is offensive is viewed not only as an effective tactic but also as the "natural" response of any "mature" person. The judge in Hampton's municipal court routinely advises disputants who appear before him to avoid one another if they cannot get along— whether this means obtaining a divorce (where spouses are concerned) or walking their dogs in opposite directions (where the parties are neighbors). In this, he clearly expresses the sentiments of the wider community. Common sense in the suburbs dictates that "normal" people will see the advantages of avoidance for the prevention and containment of conflict.

In general, people in Hampton seem to have difficulty in understanding how any group of people could favor confrontation or choose it over avoidance. It is hardly an exaggeration to conclude that the central procedural imperative of their ethical philosophy is to do as little as possible when tensions arise. Moral minimalism is thus, from the point of view of those who engage in it, not simply something thrust upon them by the conditions of modern life, but a welcome feature of their social organization. Seemingly, they would have their moral life no other way.

Conflict and Caring

Moral minimalism entails a considerable degree of indifference to the wrongdoing of others. In fact, in settings where moral minimalism dominates as it does in the suburbs, this is only one dimension of a larger indifference that is found. If people in such places cannot be bothered to take action against those who offend them or to engage in conflicts, neither can they be bothered to help those in need. Positive obligations to assist others are thus also minimal where moral minimalism flourishes.

If weak social ties generate weak social control, they undermine strong patterns of mutual aid as well. Much theoretical and empirical work has established that generosity and kindness increase with intimacy and social cohesion.[5] It therefore follows that groups in which people are atomized and separated from one another by a great deal of social distance—and where moral minimalism is likely—will not be very altruistic. This seems part of an even larger pattern in which many human activities rise and fall in intensity together. Highly dense and closely bonded groups appear to produce more music and more religion, for example, as well as more social control and altruism. One theory actually posits that culture as we know it emerged prehistorically with an increase in the average population and density of human societies.[6]

The relationship between social control and altruism has been captured in an African song recently recorded by an anthropologist:

> He who kills me, who will it be
> but my kinsman?
> He who succours me, who will it be
> but my kinsman?[7]

In contemporary America, too, most homicides and assaults occur during conflict between intimates—people also likely to assist each other in a host of difficulties.[8] At the other end of the scale, those who widely practice avoidance and other moral restraint have attracted notice for their lack of generosity. The Hadza, for example, a hunting and gathering group from Tanzania who rely heavily on avoidance to manage conflict, engage in little sharing or mutual aid:

> Among the Hadza, . . . when things go wrong, they cannot count on sustained assistance. I have discussed elsewhere the neglect and abandonment of the injured, the sick, and the dying; [this] is an integral part of a system in which individuals are not recognized as having burdensome responsibilities to others.[9]

Similarly, nineteenth-century Americans on the overland trail to the West simply separated from those who offended them; at the same time, they engaged in little altruism. If they encountered needy people in their travels, they generally showed them no charity. On the contrary, if scarcity made their own goods more valuable, they were ready to sell their possessions to the desperate at windfall prices.[10] Finally, among strangers in the modern world—where great reluctance to confront moral transgressors is found—there is likewise little willingness to come to the aid of those in need. The indifference of bystanders to one another's most urgent troubles has come to be perceived as a significant social problem, and a considerable research literature has grown up around it.[11]

In suburbia, the social environment fosters restraint in the face of grievances and, predictably, little willingness to engage in mutual aid. To an extent in families, but especially among friends and neighbors, assistance is restricted to casual actions that entail few costs. Its primary form is the small favor—picking up someone else's child after school, loaning someone a cooking ingredient or laundry detergent, shoveling someone's snow in winter, or watching someone's house while its occupants are away. True sacrifices, however, are rare, particularly outside the household. Neighbors are unlikely to share in the care of an invalid or in the carrying out of major work around someone else's house, and they essentially never give one another financial assistance of any kind.

The suburban locations where greater amounts of social control are found are precisely those where mutual aid is most available. Families contain more social control and mutual aid than neighborhoods, and neighborhoods more than public places. Young friends share more with each other than adult friends do. And, in Hampton, working-class people engage in more mutual support than middle-class people. One group of working-class siblings born in Italy pooled their incomes for years until they had managed to move each of their number—one at a time—to the United States. Once assembled on American soil, they continued to pool their resources, buying each person (beginning with the eldest) a house. Long after middle-class brothers and sisters would have scattered across the country, they were working together for the good of all. Throughout the town, the greater support which members of the Italian-American community find in their personal relationships is as widely known as their greater propensity for angry confrontation. Indeed, it appears to arouse considerable envy—or at least wistfulness—in members of the more atomized middle class.

These patterns provide a glimpse at another side of the culture of moral minimalism. People with little occasion for enmity are also unlikely to develop strong friendships. If it makes no sense to confront offenders, it correspondingly makes no sense to shower anyone with kindness. Moderation thus prevails in both positive and negative behavior alike. In this sense, weak social ties breed a general indifference and coldness, and a lack of conflict is accompanied by a lack of caring.

The Moral Order of the Future

People in the suburbs live in a world characterized by nonviolence and nonconfrontation, in which civility prevails and disturbances of the peace are uncommon. In this sense, suburbia is a model of social order. The order is not born, however, of conditions widely perceived to generate social harmony. It does not arise from intimacy and connectedness, but rather from some of the very things more often presumed to bring about conflict and violence—transiency, fragmentation, isolation, atomization, and indifference among people. The suburbs lack social cohesion but they are free of strife. They are, so to speak, disorganized and orderly at the same time.

This seeming anomaly suggests the need to revise traditional understandings about what is necessary for peace and tranquillity in human affairs. The most apparently disintegrative tendencies of modern life actually breed a harmonious social order all their own. It is ironic that the closest parallel to this disorganized order, which derives from features of society that seem especially modern, should be found among the most primitive groups of people—hunters and gatherers who are also transient and individuated and who also rely heavily on avoidance to cope with interpersonal tensions. The moral order of suburbs seems more closely linked to the future than to the past, however.

Suburbia is growing at a rapid rate. Simultaneously, rural areas and central cities are shrinking. As this happens, it appears that more and more people live in an environment characterized by transiency and fragmentation of social networks, along with spatial separation, privacy, and insulation from strangers. Increasingly, people move about freely, families scatter, and individuals are on their own, able to withdraw from others at will, without either the support or the constraint that strong social ties entail. If all this continues, moral minimalism should become an ever more pervasive feature of modern life. Suburbia may thus provide a study in the moral order of the future.

Notes

Preface

1. See Black, "Social control as a dependent variable," 1984c.

Chapter 1

1. See Hobbes, *Leviathan*; Locke, "Essay concerning civil government"; Rousseau, *Social Contract*.

2. Durkheim, *Division of Labor*; idem, *Rules of Sociological Method*, 64–75.

3. See the materials assembled in Cain and Hunt, *Marx and Engels on Law*.

4. Weber, *Law in Economy and Society*.

5. For representative collections and overviews, see Bohannan, *Law and Warfare*, 1967b; Nader and Todd, *Disputing Process*; Roberts, *Order and Dispute*.

6. See, e.g., the materials assembled in Aubert, *Sociology of Law*; Akers and Hawkins, *Law and Control*; Evan, *Sociology of Law*; Abel, *Politics of Informal Justice*; Tomasic and Feeley, *Neighborhood Justice*.

7. See especially Black, *Behavior of Law*, 1976.

8. See Suttles, *Social Order of the Slum*; Felstiner, "Influences of social organization"; Merry, "Going to court," 1979; Engel, "Legal pluralism," 1980; Thomas-Buckle and Buckle, "Doing unto others"; Baumgartner, "Social control in suburbia," 1984b; Engel, "Oven-bird's song," 1984; Baumgartner, "Law and the middle class," 1985; Ellickson, "Of Coase and cattle"; Greenhouse, *Praying for Justice*.

9. See U.S. News and World Report, "America's shrinking cities," 66.

137

10. Maloney, "America's suburbs," 60.

11. See, e.g., Godfield, "Limits of suburban growth."

12. For a general discussion of trends, see Farley, "Suburban population growth."

13. See Wilkinson, "Impact of suburbanization."

14. On these economic developments, see, e.g., Tarver, "Suburbanization of retail trade"; Leonard, "Economic aspects of suburbanization"; Chinitz, "Introduction"; Birch, Economic Future; Masotti and Hadden, *Suburbia in Transition*, 82–110; Kasarda, "Changing occupational structure."

15. There has been some interest, for example, in the "suburban captivity of the churches." See Winter, *Suburban Captivity*.

16. Maloney, "America's suburbs," 57.

17. See Schnore, "Status of cities and suburbs"; United States Advisory Commission on Intergovernmental Relations, *Metropolitan Disparities*.

18. See, e.g., Berger, *Working-Class Suburb*; Dobriner, *Class in Suburbia*; Blumberg and Lalli, "Little ghettoes"; Sobin, *Future of the American Suburbs*, 42–58.

19. Dolce, "Preface," 1976a, viii.

20. On the status characteristics of suburbs see, e.g., Duncan and Reiss, *Urban and Rural Communities*, Chapter 11; Haar, *Suburban Problems*, Chapter 2; Farley, "Suburban population growth."

21. See, e.g., Duncan and Reiss, *Urban and Rural Communities*, Chapter 11; Long and Glick, "Family patterns."

22. Carlos, "Religious participation." See also Gans, *Levittowners*, 264–266; W. Newman, "Religion in suburban America."

23. See Hausknecht, *Joiners*, 17–19. See also Seeley, Sim, and Loosley, *Crestwood Heights*, Chapter 10; Whyte, *Organization Man*, 317–318; Gans, *Levittowners*, 262–264.

24. Symons, *Evolution of Human Sexuality*, 35–36.

25. See Popenoe, *Suburban Environment*, 1977, 119. See also Gordon, Gordon, and Gunther, *Split-Level Trap*; Perrin, *Everything in Its Place*; Popenoe, *Private Pleasure, Public Plight*, 1985.

26. Margolis, *Managers*, 145.

27. On this side of suburban relationships, see Whyte, *Organization Man*, especially 329. See also Margolis, *Managers*; Wellman, "Community question."

28. On the concept of weak ties, see Granovetter, "Strength of weak ties."

29. See, e.g., Fava, "Suburbanism as a way of life," 1956; Martin, "Structuring of social relationships"; Whyte, *Organization Man*, Chap-

ters 25 and 26; Fava, "Contrasts in neighboring," 1958; Gans, *Levit-towners*, especially 261-262; Fischer and Jackson, "Suburbs, networks, and attitudes."

30. See Danielson, *Politics of Exclusion*; Dolce, *Suburbia*, 1976b; Perrin, *Everything in Its Place*.

31. This confirms a recent hypothesis that avoidance might be common in some modern settings. See Felstiner, "Influences of social organization."

32. See generally Fürer-Haimendorf, *Morals and Merit*, 17-24; Hirschman, *Exit, Voice, and Loyalty*; Felstiner, "Influences of social organization."

33. Roberts, *Order and Dispute*, 84. See also Masters, "Ostracism, voice, and exit."

34. See, respectively, Fürer-Haimendorf, *Morals and Merit*; Woodburn, "Minimal politics"; Turnbull, *Forest People*; Balikci, *Netsilik Eskimo*, 192-193.

35. Bohannan, "Introduction," 1967a, xiii.

36. See Black and Baumgartner, "Theory of the third party."

Chapter 2

1. See Glaser, "Constant comparative method," 436; see also Becker and Geer, "Participant observation and interviewing."

2. See Koch, *War and Peace in Jalémó*, 23-34.

Chapter 3

1. Nader and Todd, *Disputing Process*, 15.

2. See Black, *Behavior of Law*, 1976, 111.

3. Nader and Todd, *Disputing Process*, 15.

4. On the significance of economic dependency in conflict situations, see Blood, "Resolving family conflicts"; Black, *Behavior of Law*, 1976, 18-20.

5. Gulliver, *Disputes and Negotiations*, 1979, 3.

6. Black and Baumgartner, "Theory of the third party," 99.

7. Boulding, "Pure theory of conflict," 47.

8. On the consequences of emotional distress in the form of "mental illness" for a person's family, see Goffman, "Insanity of place," 1969; on its use as a rational way of handling conflicts with others, see Szasz, *Myth of Mental Illness*; Baumgartner, "Social control from below," 1984a, 324-

331; see also Laing and Esterson, *Sanity, Madness, and the Family*; Laing, *Politics of the Family*.

9. See, e.g., Bullock, Siegal, Weissman, and Paykel, "Weeping wife"; Weissman and Paykel, *Depressed Woman*; Horwitz, "Psychiatric help seeking," 1978.

10. Wyden, *Suburbia's Coddled Kids*, 91.

11. McLane, "Cheap Trick finds heaven," 51.

12. Cervantes, "High school dropout."

13. Wyden, *Suburbia's Coddled Kids*, 99; Richards, "Middle-class vandalism."

14. On suicide as "an aggressive and defensive weapon," see Stengal, *Suicide and Attempted Suicide*, 115–116; see also Jeffreys, "Samsonic suicide."

15. On psychiatrists as third parties, see Goffman, "Insanity of place," 1969; Black and Baumgartner, "Theory of the third party," 109–111.

16. Colson, "Spirit possession among the Tonga," 1969, 93.

17. Lewis, "Spirit possession in Somaliland," 1969, 189–190.

18. See Llewellyn and Hoebel, *Cheyenne Way*, 49, note 5; Moore, "Legal liability"; Colson, *Tradition and Contract*, 1974, 53–59.

19. See, respectively, Collier, *Law and Social Change*, 183–189; Bolton and Bolton, "Domestic quarrels among the Qolla"; Koch, *War and Peace in Jalémó*, 98–108.

20. See Fustel de Coulanges, *Ancient City*, 85–94; Nisbet, "Kinship and political power"; Arensberg and Kimball, *Family and Community in Ireland*; Rattray, *Ashanti*, 1923, Chapter 1.

21. See Sahlins, *Stone Age Economics*, 135–139.

22. See, respectively, Gibbs, "Kpelle moot"; Bohannan, *Justice and Judgment*, 1957, Chapter 9; Gulliver, "Dispute settlement without courts," 1969.

23. Benson, Brown, and Sheehy, "Survey of family difficulties."

24. This is similar to what American police do in more urban settings; see Black, *Manners and Customs*, 1980, Chapter 5; Palenski, "Mediation by police."

25. See Laslett, "The family."

26. See Town of New Haven, *Ancient Town Records*, 1917, 246–247.

27. See Baumgartner, "Law and social status," 1978.

28. See Arensberg and Kimball, *Family and Community in Ireland*, e.g., 163.

29. Gluckman, *Judicial Process*, 1967, 25.

30. See, generally, Merry, "Social organization of mediation," 1982.

31. See, e.g., Lewis, "Spirit possession and deprivation cults," 1966; Colson, "Spirit possession among the Tonga," 1969.
32. See, e.g., Szasz, *Myth of Mental Illness*; Chesler, "Women as psychiatric patients"; Gove and Tudor, "Sex roles and mental illness."
33. See Black, *Manners and Customs*, 1980, Chapter 5.
34. This is similar to what is found in the courts of the Zapotec Indians of Mexico; see Nader, "Zapotec law cases."
35. See, e.g., Goode, "Marital stability"; Monahan, "Divorce by occupational level"; Bernard, "Marital stability."
36. See Ackerman, "Affiliations"; Scanzoni, "Marital disorganization."
37. See, e.g., Scheff, "Student psychiatric clinic"; Greenley and Mechanic, "Seeking help"; Horwitz, "Therapy and social solidarity," 1984, 238–242.
38. Horwitz, *Social Control of Mental Illness*, 1982; idem, "Therapy and social solidarity," 1984.
39. See, e.g., Gottfredson and Hindelang, "The behavior of law."
40. See Black, "Common sense," 1979; see also Durkheim, *Division of Labor*, 1893, 71–73.
41. Swift, *Gulliver's Travels*, 22–23.
42. Bloch, *Feudal Society*, 296.
43. Baldick, *The Duel*, 97.
44. Straus, Gilles, and Steinmetz, *Behind Closed Doors*, 171–173.
45. Vera Institute of Justice, *Felony Arrests*, 31–32.
46. Allen, *Assault with a Deadly Weapon*, 74.
47. Edgerton, *Alone Together*, 187–188.
48. Black, *Manners and Customs*, 1980, 179.
49. Vera Institute of Justice, *Felony Arrests*, 32–33.
50. McGillis, "The quiet (r)evolution," 22–23.
51. Wolfgang, *Patterns in Criminal Homicide*, Chapter 10.
52. Ibid., 188–189.
53. Lundsgaarde, *Murder in Space City*.
54. Baumgartner, "Law and social status," 1978, 157.
55. Town of New Haven, *Records of the Colony*, 1857, 173.
56. Frake, "Litigation in Lipay," 221.
57. Ibid., 220.
58. Berman and Spindler, "Soviet comrades' courts," especially 870, 887, 888.
59. Ibid., 876.
60. Gulliver, "Dispute settlement without courts," 1969, 52–53.
61. Ibid., 57–59.

62. See Black, *Behavior of Law*, 1976, 85.

63. On this issue as it relates to conflict, see Blood, "Resolving family conflicts."

64. Starr and Yngvesson, "Scarcity and disputing."

65. Stack, *All Our Kin.*

66. See, generally, Fürer-Haimendorf, *Morals and Merit*, 17–24; Hirschman, *Exit, Voice, and Loyalty*; Felstiner, "Influences of social organization"; see also Douglas, *Natural Symbols*, Chapters 4–8.

67. Felstiner, "Influences of social organization."

68. See Roberts, *Order and Dispute*; Masters, "Ostracism, voice, and exit."

69. Stauder, "Anarchy and ecology," 163.

70. Ibid.

71. Reid, *Law for the Elephant*, Chapter 8.

72. Tanner, "Small European communities."

73. Joseph Doyle, personal communication.

74. Hirschman, *Exit, Voice, and Loyalty.*

75. Fürer-Haimendorf, *Morals and Merit*, 17–24.

76. Carneiro, "Origin of the state"; Taylor, *Community, Anarchy, and Liberty*, 135–139.

77. Bolton and Bolton, "Domestic quarrels among the Qolla," 74–75.

78. See Richer, "Economics of child-raising"; Edwards and Brauberger, "Exchange and parent-youth conflict."

79. Black, *Behavior of Law*, 41.

80. See Black and Baumgartner, "Theory of the third party," 113.

81. See Black, *Behavior of Law*, 1976, 21–30.

82. Srinivas, "Dominant caste in Rampura," 15.

83. Chang, *Chinese Gentry*, 63.

84. See, generally, Bloch, *Feudal Society.*

85. See Rothenberger, "Dispute settlement in Lebanon," 175–177.

86. Hepworth and Turner, *Confession*, 56; see also Lea, *Confession and Indulgences*, 290.

87. Hepworth and Turner, *Confession*, 56.

88. Black, Police Encounters and Social Organization, 1968, 109.

89. Schulman, *Spousal Violence.*

90. Gans, *Levittowners*, 225.

91. See Vera Institute of Justice, *Felony Arrests*, 19, 27, 67, 87, 106.

92. Hiday, "Reformed commitment procedures," 675; see also Hollingshead and Redlich, *Social Class and Mental Illness.*

93. Nader, "Zapotec law cases," 413.

Chapter 4

1. See, respectively, Pospisil, *Kapauku Papuans and their Law*; Koch, *War and Peace in Jalémó*; Harner, *Jivaro*; Chagnon, *Yanomamö*; Evans-Pritchard, *Nuer*; Lewis, *Pastoral Democracy*, 1961; Baldick, *The Duel*.

2. See, respectively, Gibbs, "Kpelle moot"; Bohannan, *Justice and Judgment*, 1957; Gulliver, *Social Control*, 1963; Ekvall, "Peace and war"; Berman, "Western legal tradition."

3. On the regulation of space and attendant privacy to control conflict in the suburbs, see Perrin, *Everything in Its Place*, Chapter 3.

4. Felstiner, "Influences of social organization"; Galanter, "Why the 'haves' come out ahead," 1974; Merry, "Going to court," 1979.

5. In a study of a suburb of Philadelphia and Trenton, it was noted that humor is a frequent vehicle through which complaints are aired. Gans, *Levittowners*, 177.

6. On the anonymous use of urban police in neighborhood conflicts, see Black, *Manners and Customs*, 1980, 116.

7. See, respectively, Todd, "Litigious marginals"; Rothenberger, "Dispute settlement in Lebanon," 160; Arensberg and Kimball, *Family and Community in Ireland*, 184–186.

8. See, e.g., Berman, "Western legal tradition"; Gibbs, "Kpelle moot."

9. See Black, "Crime as social control," 1984a.

10. All of this is consistent with the observation that in Levittown, a suburb of Philadelphia and Trenton, working-class people are more likely than middle-class people to report quarrels between their neighbors. Gans, *Levittowners*, 160.

11. See, e.g., Black, *Behavior of Law*, 1976, 16–21; but see Silberman, "Law as process."

12. See Black, *Manners and Customs*, 1980, Chapter 5.

13. Todd, "Litigious marginals."

14. Baldick, *The Duel*, 61.

15. Cohn, "Law and change," 88.

16. Jones, *Men of Influence in Nuristan*, 109.

17. Rothenberger, "Dispute settlement in Lebanon," 170–171.

18. Bloch, *Feudal Society*, 296.

19. On weak ties, see Granovetter, "Strength of weak ties."

20. On this situation in a lower-middle-class community, see Rieder, *Canarsie*, 173.

21. See Douglas, *Natural Symbols*, Chapters 4–8.

22. Fürer-Haimendorf, *Morals and Merit*, 17–24.

23. Cohen, "Who stole the rabbits?"

24. Felstiner, "Influences of social organization."
25. Black, *Behavior of Law*, 1976, Chapter 7.
26. Ibid., 111.
27. Ibid., 118–119.
28. See, e.g., Rattray, *Ashanti Law and Constitution*, 1929, 37; Hoebel, *Law of Primitive Man*, 88–92; Werthman and Piliavin, "Gang members and the police"; Farrell and Swigert, "Self-fulfilling prophecy."
29. Gluckman, *Judicial Process*, 1967, 21–22.
30. Colson, *Tradition and Contract*, 1974, 53–59; see also Black, *Behavior of Law*, 1976, 137.
31. Christie, "Conflicts as property," 6.
32. Bourdieu, "The sentiment of honour," 212.
33. Frake, "Litigation in Lipay," 221.
34. Matza and Sykes, "Juvenile delinquency and subterranean values."
35. See, e.g., Straus, Gelles, and Steinmetz, *Behind Closed Doors*, 149–151.
36. Thoden van Velzen and van Wetering, "Intra-societal aggression."
37. Gulliver, "Dispute settlement without courts," 1969; see also Bohannan, *Justice and Judgment*, 1957, 65.
38. See Black, *Behavior of Law*, 1976, Chapter 4.
39. Chroust, "Legal profession in ancient Athens," especially 352–353.
40. See Black, *Behavior of Law*, 1976, Chapter 1.

Chapter 5

1. See, e.g., Jackson, "Effect of suburbanization," 104–105; Popenoe, *Suburban Environment*, 1977; idem, "Urban sprawl," 1979.
2. See Black, *The Behavior of Law*, 1976, 40–41.
3. See, e.g., Simmel, "The stranger," 1908b; Shack and Skinner, *Strangers in African Society*.
4. This is true in other suburbs as well. See, e.g., Danielson, *Politics of Exclusion*; Dolce, *Suburbia*, 1976b; Perrin, *Everything in Its Place*.
5. See, e.g., Goffman, *Behavior in Public Places*, 1963.
6. For a similar pattern in a high crime rate area, see Merry, *Urban Danger*, 1981.
7. Black and Baumgartner, "Theory of the third party," 95–97.
8. See Silver, "Demand for order."
9. See McCausland, "Crime in the suburbs."
10. See Campbell and Schuman, "Black and white experience," 109.

11. See J. Q. Wilson, *Varieties of Police Behavior.*
12. Durkheim, *Rules of Sociological Method,* 1895, 68–69.
13. Erikson, *Wayward Puritans,* 26.
14. See, e.g., Wyden, *Suburbia's Coddled Kids,* 102–103; Gans, *Levittowners,* 213.
15. The high proportion of informal outcomes accords with practices in other suburbs. See Loth, *Crime in the Suburbs,* 124–126; J. Q. Wilson, *Varieties of Police Behavior.*
16. Data supplied by Donald Black.
17. See O. Newman, *Defensible Space;* see also Merry, *Urban Danger,* 1981.
18. Wilson and Boland, "Effect of the police."
19. Ibid.
20. National Safety Council, *Accident Facts,* 46.
21. See Christie, "Conflicts as property."
22. Abel, "Western courts," 1979, 171–175.
23. See Rieder, *Canarsie,* 71; Rudel, "Crowds."
24. Milgram, "Experience of living in cities."
25. Lofland, *A World of Strangers,* 151–155.
26. Edgerton, *Alone Together.*

Chapter 6

1. See, e.g., Graham and Gurr, "Introduction"; Ehrlich, "Legal pollution"; Manning, "Hyperlexis."
2. See, respectively, Thomas-Buckle and Buckle, "Doing unto others"; Engel, "Oven-bird's song," 1984; Ellickson, "Of Coase and cattle"; Greenhouse, *Praying for Justice.*
3. See Galanter, "Reading the landscape of disputes," 1984; Black, "Jurocracy in America," 1984b.
4. See, e.g., Simmel, "Conflict," 1908a; Coser, *Functions of Social Conflict;* Christie, "Conflicts as property."
5. See, e.g., Sahlins, *Stone Age Economics,* Chapter 5; Bar-Tal, *Prosocial Behavior,* 79; compare E. O. Wilson, *Sociobiology,* Chapter 5.
6. Pfeiffer, *Creative Explosion.*
7. Gluckman, "Moral crisis," 1972, 5.
8. See Wolfgang, *Patterns in Criminal Homicide,* Chapter 11.
9. Woodburn, "Minimal politics," 260.
10. Reid, *Law for the Elephant,* Chapter 3.
11. See Latané and Darley, *Unresponsive Bystander.*

References

Abel, Richard L.
  1979   "Western courts in non-western settings: patterns of court use
          in colonial and neo-colonial Africa." Pages 167–200 in *The
          Imposition of Law*, edited by Sandra B. Burman and Barbara E.
          Harrell-Bond. New York: Academic Press.
Abel, Richard L. (editor)
  1982   *The Politics of Informal Justice*. New York: Academic Press.
Ackerman, Charles
  1963   "Affiliations: structural determinants of differential divorce
          rates." *American Journal of Sociology* 69:13–20.
Akers, Ronald L., and Richard Hawkins (editors)
  1975   *Law and Control in Society*. Englewood Cliffs: Prentice-Hall.
Allen, John
  1977   *Assault with a Deadly Weapon: The Autobiography of a Street
          Criminal*, edited by Dianne Hall Kelly and Philip Heymann.
          New York: McGraw-Hill.
Arensberg, Conrad M., and Solon T. Kimball
  1968   *Family and Community in Ireland*. Cambridge: Harvard Uni-
          versity Press (second edition; first edition, 1940).
Aubert, Vilhelm (editor)
  1969   *Sociology of Law: Selected Readings*. Baltimore: Penguin
          Books.
Baldick, Robert
  1965   *The Duel: A History of Duelling*. London: Chapman and Hall.
Balikci, Asen
  1970   *The Netsilik Eskimo*. Garden City: Natural History Press.

Bar-Tal, Daniel
1976   *Prosocial Behavior: Theory and Research*. Washington: Hemisphere Publishing Corporation.

Baumgartner, M. P.
1978   "Law and social status in colonial New Haven, 1639-1665." Pages 153-174 in *Research in Law and Sociology: An Annual Compilation of Research*, Volume 1, edited by Rita J. Simon. Greenwich: JAI Press.

1984a   "Social control from below." Pages 303-345 in *Toward a General Theory of Social Control*, Volume 1: *Fundamentals*, edited by Donald Black. Orlando: Academic Press.

1984b   "Social control in suburbia." Pages 79-103 in *Toward a General Theory of Social Control*, Volume 2: *Selected Problems*, edited by Donald Black. Orlando: Academic Press.

1985   "Law and the middle class: evidence from a suburban town." *Law and Human Behavior* 9:3-24.

Becker, Howard S., and Blanche Geer
1957   "Participant observation and interviewing: a comparison." *Human Organization* 16:28-32.

Benson, Purnell H., Arlo Brown, Jr., and Sister Loretta Maria Sheehy
1956   "A survey of family difficulties in a metropolitan suburb." *Marriage and Family Living* 18:249-253.

Berger, Bennett M.
1960   *Working-Class Suburb: A Study of Auto Workers in Suburbia*. Berkeley: University of California Press.

Berman, Harold J.
1978   "The background of the western legal tradition in the folklaw of the peoples of Europe." *University of Chicago Law Review* 45:553-597.

Berman, Harold J., and James W. Spindler
1963   "Soviet comrades' courts." *Washington Law Review* 38:842-910.

Bernard, Jessie
1966   "Marital stability and patterns of status variables." *Journal of Marriage and the Family* 28:421-439.

Birch, David L.
1970   The Economic Future of City and Suburb. CED Supplementary Paper Number 30. Published by the Committee for Economic Development.

Black, Donald
1968   Police Encounters and Social Organization: An Observation

Study. Unpublished doctoral dissertation, Department of Sociology, University of Michigan.

1976   *The Behavior of Law.* New York: Academic Press.

1979   "Common sense in the sociology of law." *American Sociological Review* 44:18–27.

1980   *The Manners and Customs of the Police.* New York: Academic Press.

1984a   "Crime as social control." Pages 1–27 in *Toward a General Theory of Social Control,* Volume 2: *Selected Problems,* edited by Donald Black. Orlando: Academic Press.

1984b   "Jurocracy in America." *The Tocqueville Review/La Revue Tocqueville* 6:273–281.

1984c   "Social control as a dependent variable." Pages 1–36 in *Toward a General Theory of Social Control,* Volume 1: *Fundamentals,* edited by Donald Black. Orlando: Academic Press.

Black, Donald, and M. P. Baumgartner

1983   "Toward a theory of the third party." Pages 84–114 in *Empirical Theories about Courts,* edited by Keith O. Boyum and Lynn Mather. New York: Longman.

Bloch, Maurice

1940   *Feudal Society,* Volume 2: *Social Classes and Political Organization.* Chicago: Phoenix Books, 1964.

Blood, Robert O., Jr.

1960   "Resolving family conflicts." *Journal of Conflict Resolution* 4:209–219.

Blumberg, Leonard, and Michael Lalli

1966   "Little ghettoes: a study of Negroes in the suburbs." *Phylon* 27:117–131.

Bohannan, Paul

1957   *Justice and Judgment among the Tiv.* London: Oxford University Press.

1967a   "Introduction." Pages xi–xiv in *Law and Warfare: Studies in the Anthropology of Conflict.* Garden City: Natural History Press.

Bohannan, Paul (editor)

1967b   *Law and Warfare: Studies in the Anthropology of Conflict.* Garden City: Natural History Press.

Bolton, Ralph, and Charlene Bolton

1973   "Domestic quarrels among the Qolla." Paper presented at the 72nd Annual Meeting of the American Anthropological Association, New Orleans, October, 1973. Published in Spanish as

Conflictos en la Familia Andina. Cuzco, Peru: Centro de Estu-
dios Andinos, 1975.

Boulding, Kenneth
1964   "A pure theory of conflict applied to organizations." Pages 41-
49 in *The Frontiers of Management Psychology*, edited by
George Fisk. New York: Harper and Row.

Bourdieu, Pierre
"The sentiment of honour in Kabyle society." Pages 193-241
in *Honour and Shame: The Values of Mediterranean Society*,
edited by J. G. Peristiany. Chicago: University of Chicago
Press.

Bullock, Ruth, Rose Siegal, Myrna Weissman, and E. S. Paykel
1972   "The weeping wife: marital relations of depressed women."
Journal of Marriage and the Family 24:488-495.

Cain, Maureen, and Alan Hunt
1979   *Marx and Engels on Law.* London: Academic Press.

Campbell, Angus, and Howard Schuman
1972   "A comparison of black and white experience in the city."
Pages 97-110 in *The End of Innocence: A Suburban Reader*,
edited by Charles M. Haar. Glenview: Scott, Foresman, and
Company.

Carlos, Serge
1970   "Religious participation and the urban-suburban continuum."
American Journal of Sociology 75:742-759.

Carneiro, Robert L.
1970   "A theory of the origin of the state." *Science* 169:733-738.

Cervantes, Lucius
1975   "Family background, primary relationships, and the high
school dropout." *Journal of Marriage and the Family* 27:218-
223.

Chagnon, Napolean A.
1977   *Yanomamö: The Fierce People.* New York: Holt, Rinehart,
and Winston (second edition; first edition, 1968).

Chang, Chung-li
1958   *The Chinese Gentry: Studies on Their Role in Nineteenth-
Century Chinese Society.* Seattle: University of Washington
Press.

Chesler, Phyllis
1971   "Women as psychiatric and psychotherapeutic patients." *Journal of Marriage and the Family* 33:746-759.

Chinitz, Benjamin
  1964   "Introduction: city and suburb." Pages 3-50 in *City and Sub-urb: The Economics of Metropolitan Growth*, edited by B. Chinitz. Englewood Cliffs: Prentice-Hall.
Christie, Nils
  1977   "Conflicts as property." *British Journal of Criminology* 17:1-15.
Chroust, Anton-Hermann
  1954   "The legal profession in ancient Athens." *Notre Dame Lawyer* 29:339-389.
Cohen, Eugene
  1972   "Who stole the rabbits?: crime, dispute, and social control in an Italian village." *Anthropological Quarterly* 45:1-14.
Cohn, Bernard S.
  1959   "Notes on law and change in North India." *Economic Development and Cultural Change* 8:79-93.
Collier, Jane Fishburne
  1973   *Law and Social Change in Zinacantan*. Stanford: Stanford University Press.
Colson, Elizabeth
  1969   "Spirit possession among the Tonga of Zambia." Pages 69-103 in *Spirit Mediumship and Society in Africa*, edited by John Beattie and John Middleton. New York: Africana Publishing Corporation.
  1974   *Tradition and Contract: The Problem of Order*. Chicago: Aldine Press.
Coser, Lewis A.
  1956   *The Functions of Social Conflict*. Glencoe: Free Press.
Danielson, Michael N.
  1976   *The Politics of Exclusion*. New York: Columbia University Press.
Dobriner, William M.
  1963   *Class in Suburbia*. Englewood Cliffs: Prentice-Hall.
Dolce, Philip C.
  1976a   "Preface." Pages vii-ix in *Suburbia: The American Dream and Dilemma*, edited by P. Dolce. Garden City: Anchor Books.
Dolce, Philip C. (editor)
  1976b   *Suburbia: The American Dream and Dilemma*. Garden City: Anchor Books.
Douglas, Mary
  1970   *Natural Symbols: Explorations in Cosmology*. New York: Pantheon Books.

Duncan, Otis Dudley, and Albert J. Reiss, Jr.
  1956   *Social Characteristics of Urban and Rural Communities, 1950.*
          New York: John Wiley and Sons.
Durkheim, Emile
  1893   *The Division of Labor in Society.* New York: Free Press, 1964.
  1895   *The Rules of Sociological Method.* New York: Free Press,
          1964.
Edgerton, Robert B.
  1979   *Alone Together: Social Order on an Urban Beach.* Los An-
          geles: University of California Press.
Edwards, John N., and Mary Ball Brauberger
  1973   "Exchange and parent-youth conflict." *Journal of Marriage and
          the Family* 35:101-107.
Ehrlich, Thomas
  1976   "Legal pollution." *New York Times Magazine* (Febru-
          ary 8):17 ff.
Ekvall, Robert B.
  1964   "Peace and war among the Tibetan nomads." *American An-
          thropologist* 66:1119-1148.
Ellickson, Robert C.
  1986   "Of Coase and cattle: dispute resolution among neighbors in
          Shasta county." *Stanford Law Review* 38:623-687.
Engel, David M.
  1980   "Legal pluralism in an American community: perspectives on
          a civil trial court." *American Bar Foundation Research Journal*
          1980:425-454.
  1984   "The oven-bird's song: insiders, outsiders, and personal inju-
          ries in an American community." *Law and Society Review*
          18:551-582.
Erikson, Kai T.
  1966   *Wayward Puritans: A Study in the Sociology of Deviance.* New
          York: John Wiley and Sons.
Evan, William M.
  1980   *The Sociology of Law: A Social-Structural Perspective.* New
          York: Free Press.
Evans-Pritchard, E. E.
  1940   *The Nuer.* London: Oxford University Press.
Farley, Reynolds
  1976   "Components of suburban population growth." Pages 3-38 in
          The Changing Face of the Suburbs, edited by Barry Schwartz.
          Chicago: University of Chicago Press.

Farrell, Ronald A., and Victoria Lynn Swigert
1978 "Prior offense as a self-fulfilling prophecy." *Law and Society Review* 12:437–453.

Fava, Sylvia Fleis
1956 "Suburbanism as a way of life." *American Sociological Review* 21:34–37.
1958 "Contrasts in neighboring: New York City and a suburban county." Pages 122–131 in *The Suburban Community*, edited by William M. Dobriner. New York: G. P. Putnam's Sons.

Felstiner, William L. F.
1974 "Influences of social organization on dispute processing." *Law and Society Review* 9:63–94.

Fischer, Claude S., and Robert Max Jackson
1976 "Suburbs, networks, and attitudes." Pages 279–307 in *The Changing Face of the Suburbs*, edited by Barry Schwartz. Chicago: University of Chicago Press.

Frake, Charles O.
1963 "Litigation in Lipay: a study in Subanun law." *Proceedings of the Ninth Pacific Science Conference* 3:217–222.

Fürer-Haimendorf, Christoph von
1967 *Morals and Merit: A Study of Values and Social Controls in South Asian Societies.* Chicago: University of Chicago Press.

Fustel de Coulanges, Numa Denis
1864 *The Ancient City: A Study on the Religion, Laws, and Institutions of Greece and Rome.* Garden City: Anchor Books, 1956.

Galanter, Marc
1974 "Why the 'haves' come out ahead: speculations on the limits of legal change." *Law and Society Review* 9:95–160.
1984 "Reading the landscape of disputes: what we know and don't know (and think we know) about our allegedly contentious and litigious society." *UCLA Law Review* 31:4–71.

Gans, Herbert J.
1967 *The Levittowners: Ways of Life and Politics in a New Suburban Community.* New York: Vintage Books.

Gibbs, James L., Jr.
1963 "The Kpelle moot: a therapeutic model for the informal settlement of disputes." *Africa* 33:1–10.

Glaser, Barney
1965 "The constant comparative method of qualitative analysis." *Social Problems* 12:436–445.

Gluckman, Max
1967   *The Judicial Process among the Barotse of Northern Rhodesia.*
        Manchester: Manchester University Press (second edition;
        first edition, 1955).
1972   "Moral crises: magical and secular solutions." Pages 1-50 in
        The Allocation of Responsibility, edited by M. Gluckman.
        Manchester: Manchester University Press.
Godfield, David R.
1976   "The limits of suburban growth: the Washington, D.C.
        SMSA." *Urban Affairs Quarterly* 12:83-101.
Goffman, Erving
1963   *Behavior in Public Places: Notes on the Social Organization of
        Gatherings.* New York: Free Press.
1969   "The insanity of place." Pages 335-390 in *Relations in Public:
        Microstudies of the Public Order.* New York: Basic Books,
        1971.
Goode, William J.
1951   "Economic factors and marital stability." *American Sociologi-
        cal Review* 16:803-812.
Gordon, Richard E., Katherine K. Gordon, and Max Gunther
1960   *The Split-Level Trap.* New York: Bernard Geis Associates.
Gottfredson, Michael R., and Michael J. Hindelang
1979   "A study of the behavior of law." *American Sociological Re-
        view* 44:3-18.
Gove, Walter R., and Jeannette F. Tudor
1973   "Adult sex roles and mental illness." *American Journal of
        Sociology* 78:812-835.
Graham, Hugh Davis, and Ted Robert Gurr
1969   "Introduction." Pages xxv-xxxii in *Violence in America: His-
        torical and Comparative Perspectives.* New York: Bantam
        Books.
Granovetter, Mark S.
1973   "The strength of weak ties." *American Journal of Sociology*
        78:1360-1380.
Greenhouse, Carol J.
1986   *Praying for Justice: Faith, Order, and Community in an Ameri-
        can Town.* Ithaca: Cornell University Press.
Greenley, James R., and David Mechanic
1976   "Social selection in seeking help for psychological prob-
        lems." *Journal of Health and Social Behavior* 17:249-
        262.

Gulliver, Philip H.
1963   *Social Control in an African Society: A Study of the Arusha,*
        Agricultural Masai of Northern Tanganyika. Boston: Boston
        University Press.
1969   "Dispute settlement without courts: The Ndendeuli of south-
        ern Tanzania." Pages 24–68 in *Law in Culture and Society,*
        edited by Laura Nader. Chicago: Aldine Press.
1979   *Disputes and Negotiations: A Cross-Cultural Perspective.*
        New York: Academic Press.
Haar, Charles M. (editor)
1974   *The President's Task Force on Suburban Problems: Final Re-*
        port. Cambridge: Ballinger Publishing Company.
Harner, Michael J.
1972   *The Jivaro: People of the Sacred Waterfalls.* Garden City:
        Anchor Books.
Hausknecht, Murray
1962   *The Joiners: A Sociological Description of Voluntary Associa-*
        tion Membership in the United States. New York: Bedminster
        Press.
Hepworth, Mike, and Bryan S. Turner
1982   *Confession: Studies in Deviance and Religion.* London: Rout-
        ledge and Kegan Paul.
Hiday, Virginia A.
1977   "Reformed commitment procedures: an empirical study in the
        courtroom." *Law and Society Review* 11:651–666.
Hirschman, Albert O.
1970   *Exit, Voice, and Loyalty: Responses to Decline in Firms, Or-*
        ganizations, and States. Cambridge: Harvard University Press.
Hobbes, Thomas
1651   *Leviathan.* Chicago: Encyclopedia Britannica, 1952.
Hoebel, E. Adamson
1954   *The Law of Primitive Man: A Study in Comparative Legal*
        Dynamics. Cambridge: Harvard University Press.
Hollingshead, August B., and Frederick C. Redlich
1958   *Social Class and Mental Illness: A Community Study.* New
        York: John Wiley and Sons.
Horwitz, Allan V.
1978   "Family, kin, and friend networks in psychiatric help seeking."
        Social Science and Medicine 12:297–304.
1982   *The Social Control of Mental Illness.* New York: Academic
        Press.

1984   "Therapy and social solidarity." Pages 211–250 in *Toward a General Theory of Social Control*, Volume 1: *Fundamentals*, edited by Donald Black. Orlando: Academic Press.

Jackson, Kenneth T.
1976   "The effect of suburbanization on the cities." Pages 89–110 in *Suburbia: The American Dream and Dilemma*, edited by Philip C. Dolce. Garden City: Anchor Books.

Jeffreys, M. D. W.
1952   "Samsonic suicide or suicide of revenge among Africans." *African Studies* 11:118–122.

Jones, Schuyler
1974   *Men of Influence in Nuristan: A Study of Social Control and Dispute Settlement in Waigal Valley, Afghanistan.* London: Seminar Press.

Kasarda, John D.
1976   "The changing occupational structure of the American metropolis: apropos the urban problem." Pages 113–136 in *The Changing Face of the Suburbs*, edited by Barry Schwartz. Chicago: University of Chicago Press.

Koch, Klaus-Friedrich
1974   *War and Peace in Jalémó: The Management of Conflict in Highland New Guinea.* Cambridge: Harvard University Press.

Laing, R. D.
1969   *The Politics of the Family and Other Essays.* New York: Pantheon Books.

Laing, R. D., and A. Esterson
1964   *Sanity, Madness and the Family: Families of Schizophrenics.* Baltimore: Penguin Books, 1970.

Laslett, Barbara
1973   "The family as a public and private institution: an historical perspective." *Journal of Marriage and the Family* 35:480–492.

Latané, Bibb, and John M. Darley
1970   *The Unresponsive Bystander: Why Doesn't He Help?* New York: Appleton-Century-Crofts.

Lea, Henry Charles
1896   *A History of Auricular Confession and Indulgences in the Latin Church.* Volume 1. London: Swan Sonnenschein.

Leonard, William N.
1958   "Economic aspects of suburbanization." Pages 181–194 in *The Suburban Community*, edited by William M. Dobriner. New York: G. P. Putnam's Sons.

Lewis, I. M.
1961   *A Pastoral Democracy: A Study of Pastoralism and Politics among the Northern Somali of the Horn of Africa.* London: Oxford University Press.
1966   "Spirit possession and deprivation cults." *Man* 1:307–329.
1969   "Spirit possession in northern Somaliland." Pages 188–219 in *Spirit Mediumship and Society in Africa,* edited by John Beattie and John Middleton. New York: Africana Publishing Corporation.

Llewellyn, Karl N., and E. Adamson Hoebel
1941   *The Cheyenne Way: Conflict and Case Law in Primitive Jurisprudence.* Norman: University of Oklahoma Press.

Locke, John
1690   "An essay concerning the true original extent and end of civil government." Book II of *Two Treatises of Civil Government.* London: J. M. Dent and Sons, 1924.

Lofland, Lyn H.
1973   *A World of Strangers: Order and Action in Urban Public Space.* New York: Basic Books.

Long, Larry H., and Paul C. Glick
1976   "Family patterns in suburban areas: recent trends." Pages 39–67 in *The Changing Face of the Suburbs,* edited by Barry Schwartz. Chicago: University of Chicago Press.

Loth, David
1967   *Crime in the Suburbs.* New York: William Morrow and Company.

Lundsgaarde, Henry P.
1977   *Murder in Space City: A Cultural Analysis of Houston Homicide Patterns.* New York: Oxford University Press.

Maloney, Lawrence D.
1984   "America's suburbs still alive and doing fine." *U.S. News and World Report* 96 (March 12):59–62.

Manning, Bayless
1977   "Hyperlexis: our national disease." *Northwestern University Law Review* 71:767–782.

Margolis, Diane Rothbard
1979   *The Managers: Corporate Life in America.* New York: William Morrow.

Martin, Walter T.
1956   "The structuring of social relationships engendered by suburban residence." *American Sociological Review* 21:446–453.

Masotti, Louis H., and Jeffrey K. Hadden (editors)
1974   *Suburbia in Transition.* New York: New Viewpoints.
Masters, Roger D.
1983   "Ostracism, voice, and exit: the biology of social participation."
        Paper presented at the Annual Meeting of the Law and Society
        Association, June, 1983.
Matza, David, and Gresham M. Sykes
1961   "Juvenile delinquency and subterranean values." *American So-
        ciological Review* 26:712–719.
McCausland, John L.
1972   "Crime in the suburbs." Pages 61–64 in *The End of Innocence:
        A Suburban Reader,* edited by Charles M. Haar. Glenview:
        Scott, Foresman, and Company.
McGillis, Daniel
1980   "The quiet (r)evolution in American dispute settlement." *Har-
        vard Law School Bulletin* 31:20–25.
McLane, Daisann
1979   "Cheap Trick finds heaven: Japan surrenders to Rick-ka, Bu-
        neee, Tom-ma and Ro-been." *Rolling Stone* Number 293
        (June 14):48–53.
Merry, Sally Engle
1979   "Going to court: strategies of dispute management in an
        American urban neighborhood." *Law and Society Review*
        13:891–925.
1981   *Urban Danger: Life in a Neighborhood of Strangers.* Philadel-
        phia: Temple University Press.
1982   "The social organization of mediation in nonindustrial so-
        cieties: implications for informal community justice in
        America." Pages 17–45 in *The Politics of Informal Justice,*
        Volume 2: *Comparative Studies,* edited by Richard L. Abel.
        New York: Academic Press.
Milgram, Stanley
1970   "The experience of living in cities." *Science* 167
        (March 13):1461–1468.
Monahan, Thomas P.
1955   "Divorce by occupational level." *Journal of Marriage and the
        Family* 17:322–324.
Moore, Sally F.
1972   "Legal liability and evolutionary interpretation: some as-
        pects of strict liability, self-help and collective responsi-
        bility." Pages 51–107 in *The Allocation of Responsibility,*

edited by Max Gluckman. Manchester: Manchester University Press.

Nader, Laura
1964 "An analysis of Zapotec law cases." *Ethnology* 3:404–419.

Nader, Laura, and Harry F. Todd, Jr. (editors)
1978 *The Disputing Process: Law in Ten Societies.* New York: Columbia University Press.

National Safety Council
1978 *Accident Facts, 1978 Edition.* Chicago: National Safety Council.

Newman, Oscar
1972 *Defensible Space: Crime Prevention through Urban Design.* New York: Macmillan.

Newman, William M.
1976 "Religion in suburban America." Pages 265–278 in *The Changing Face of the Suburbs,* edited by Barry Schwartz. Chicago: University of Chicago Press.

Nisbet, Robert
1964 "Kinship and political power in first century Rome." Pages 257–271 in *Sociology and History,* edited by Werner J. Cahnman and Alvin Boskoff. New York: Free Press.

Palenski, Joseph E.
1984 "The use of mediation by police." Pages 31–38 in *Community Mediation,* edited by J. A. Lemmon. *Mediation Quarterly,* Number 5. San Francisco: Jossey-Bass.

Perrin, Constance
1977 *Everything in Its Place: Social Order and Land Use in America.* Princeton: Princeton University Press.

Pfeiffer, John E.
1982 *The Creative Explosion: An Inquiry into the Origins of Art and Religion.* Ithaca: Cornell University Press.

Popenoe, David
1977 *The Suburban Environment: Sweden and the United States.* Chicago: University of Chicago Press.
1979 "Urban sprawl: some neglected sociological considerations." *Sociology and Social Research* 63:255–268.
1985 *Private Pleasure, Public Plight: American Metropolitan Community Life in Comparative Perspective.* New Brunswick: Transaction Books.

Pospisil, Leopold
1958 *Kapauku Papuans and Their Law.* New Haven: Yale University Publications in Anthropology, Number 54.

Rattray, R. S.
   1923   *Ashanti.* Oxford: Clarendon Press.
   1929   *Ashanti Law and Constitution.* Oxford: Clarendon Press.
Reid, John Phillip
   1980   *Law for the Elephant: Property and Social Behavior on the Overland Trail.* San Marino: The Huntingdon Library.
Richards, Pamela
   1979   "Middle-class vandalism and age-status conflict." *Social Problems* 26:482–497.
Richer, Stephen
   1968   "The economics of child-raising." *Journal of Marriage and the Family* 30:462–466.
Rieder, Jonathan
   1985   *Canarsie: The Jews and Italians of Brooklyn against Liberalism.* Cambridge: Harvard University Press.
Roberts, Simon
   1979   *Order and Dispute: An Introduction to Legal Anthropology.* Baltimore: Penguin Books.
Rothenberger, John E.
   1978   "The social dynamics of dispute settlement in a Sunni Muslim village in Lebanon." Pages 152–180 in *The Disputing Process: Law in Ten Societies,* edited by Laura Nader and Harry F. Todd, Jr. New York: Columbia University Press.
Rousseau, Jean-Jacques
   1762   *The Social Contract: Or Principles of Political Right.* Chicago: Encyclopedia Britannica, 1952.
Rudel, T. K.
   1985   "Crowds and strategies for avoiding them in a densely settled region." *Environment and Planning* 17:815–828.
Sahlins, Marshall
   1972   *Stone Age Economics.* Chicago: Aldine Press.
Scanzoni, John
   1965   "A reinquiry into marital disorganization." *Journal of Marriage and the Family* 27:483–491.
Scheff, Thomas J.
   1966   "Users and non-users of a student psychiatric clinic." *Journal of Health and Human Behavior* 7:114–121.
Schnore, Leo F.
   1963   "The socio-economic status of cities and suburbs." *American Sociological Review* 28:76–85.

Schulman, Mark A.
1979   *A Survey of Spousal Violence against Women in Kentucky.*
        Washington: United States Department of Justice.
Seeley, John R., R. Alexander Sim, and Elizabeth W. Loosley
1956   *Crestwood Heights: A Study of the Culture of Suburban Life.*
        New York: Basic Books.
Shack, William A., and Elliott P. Skinner
1979   *Strangers in African Society.* Berkeley: University of California
        Press.
Silberman, Matthew
1977   "Law as process: a value-added model of the mobilization of
        law." Paper presented at the 72nd Annual Meeting of the
        American Sociological Association, September, 1977.
Silver, Allan
1966   "The demand for order in civil society: a review of some
        themes in the history of urban crime, police, and riot." Pages
        1-24 in *The Police: Six Sociological Essays,* edited by David J.
        Bordua. New York: John Wiley and Sons.
Simmel, Georg
1908a   "Conflict." Pages 11-123 in *Conflict and the Web of Group
        Affiliations.* Glencoe: Free Press, 1955.
1908b   "The stranger." Pages 402-408 in *The Sociology of Georg
        Simmel,* edited by Kurt H. Wolff. New York: Free Press,
        1950.
Sobin, Dennis P.
1971   *The Future of the American Suburbs: Survival or Extinction?*
        Port Washington: National University Publications, Kennikat
        Press.
Srinivas, M. N.
1959   "The dominant caste in Rampura." *American Anthropologist*
        61:1-16.
Stack, Carol
1974   *All Our Kin: Strategies for Survival in a Black Community.*
        New York: Harper and Row.
Starr, June, and Barbara Yngvesson
1975   "Scarcity and disputing: zeroing in on compromise decisions."
        American Ethnologist 2:553-566.
Stauder, Jack
1972   "Anarchy and ecology: political society among the Majangir."
        Southwestern Journal of Anthropology 28:153-168.

162   References

Stengal, Erwin
1964   *Suicide and Attempted Suicide.* Baltimore: Penguin Books.
Straus, Murray A., Richard J. Gelles, and Suzanne K. Steinmetz
1980   *Behind Closed Doors: Violence in the American Family.*
Garden City: Anchor Books, 1981.
Suttles, Gerald D.
1968   *The Social Order of the Slum: Ethnicity and Territory in the Inner City.* Chicago: University of Chicago Press.
Swift, Jonathan
1726   *Gulliver's Travels.* Chicago: Encyclopedia Britannica, 1952.
Symons, Donald
1979   *The Evolution of Human Sexuality.* New York: Oxford University Press.
Szasz, Thomas S.
1961   *The Myth of Mental Illness: Foundations of a Theory of Personal Conduct.* New York: Harper and Row.
Tanner, R. E. S.
1965   "Conflict within small European communities in Tanganyika." *Human Organization* 24:319–327.
Tarver, James D.
1957   "Suburbanization of retail trade in the standard metropolitan areas of the United States, 1948–54." *American Sociological Review* 22:429–433.
Taylor, Michael
1982   *Community, Anarchy and Liberty.* Cambridge: Cambridge University Press.
Thoden van Velzen, H. U. E., and W. van Wetering
1960   "Residence, power groups and intra-societal aggression: an enquiry into the conditions leading to peacefulness within nonstratified societies." *International Archives of Ethnography* 49 (Part 2):169–200.
Thomas-Buckle, Suzann, and Leonard Buckle
1982   "Doing unto others: disputes and dispute processing in an urban American neighborhood." Pages 78–90 in *Neighborhood Justice: Assessment of an Emerging Idea,* edited by Roman Tomasic and Malcolm M. Feeley. New York: Longman.
Todd, Harry F., Jr.
1978   "Litigious marginals: character and disputing in a Bavarian village." Pages 86–121 in *The Disputing Process: Law in Ten Societies,* edited by Laura Nader and Harry F. Todd, Jr. New York: Columbia University Press.

Tomasic, Roman, and Malcolm M. Feeley (editors)
1982 *Neighborhood Justice: Assessment of an Emerging Idea.* New York: Longman.

Town of New Haven
1857 *Records of the Colony and Plantation of New Haven from 1638 to 1649,* transcribed and edited in accordance with a resolution of the General Assembly of Connecticut by Charles J. Hoadly. Hartford: Case, Tiffany and Company.
1917 *Ancient Town Records,* Volume 1: *New Haven Town Records 1649-1662.* Edited by Franklin Bowditch Dexter for the New Haven Colony Historical Society. New Haven: Printed for the Society.

Turnbull, Colin M.
1961 *The Forest People.* New York: Simon and Schuster.

United States Advisory Commission on Intergovernmental Relations
1965 *Metropolitan Social and Economic Disparities: Implications for Intergovernmental Relations in Central Cities and Suburbs.* Washington: U.S. Government Printing Office.

U.S. News and World Report
1981 "Tale of America's shrinking cities." Volume 90 (March 23):66.

Vera Institute of Justice
1977 *Felony Arrests: Their Prosecution and Disposition in New York City's Courts.* New York: Vera Institute of Justice.

Weber, Max
1925 *Max Weber on Law in Economy and Society,* edited by Max Rheinstein. Cambridge: Harvard University Press, 1966.

Weissman, Myrna, and Eugene S. Paykel
1974 *The Depressed Woman: A Study of Social Relationships.* Chicago: University of Chicago Press.

Wellman, Barry
1979 "The community question: the intimate networks of East Yorkers." *American Journal of Sociology* 84:1201-1231.

Werthman, Carl, and Irving Piliavin
1967 "Gang members and the police." Pages 56-98 in *The Police: Six Sociological Essays,* edited by David J. Bordua. New York: John Wiley and Sons.

Whyte, William H., Jr.
1956 *The Organization Man.* New York: Simon and Schuster.

Wilkinson, Pierce B.
1976 "The impact of suburbanization on government and politics in

contemporary America." Pages 59–87 in *Suburbia: The American Dream and Dilemma*, edited by Philip C. Dolce. Garden City: Anchor Books.

Wilson, Edward O.
1975   *Sociobiology: The New Synthesis.* Cambridge: Belknap Press.

Wilson, James Q.
1968   *Varieties of Police Behavior: The Management of Law and Order in Eight Communities.* Cambridge: Harvard University Press.

Wilson, James Q., and Barbara Boland
1978   "The effect of the police on crime." *Law and Society Review* 12:367–390.

Winter, Gibson
1961   *The Suburban Captivity of the Churches: An Analysis of Protestant Responsibility in the Expanding Metropolis.* New York: Doubleday.

Wolfgang, Marvin E.
1958   *Patterns in Criminal Homicide.* New York: John Wiley and Sons.

Woodburn, James
1979   "Minimal politics: the political organization of the Hadza of north Tanzania." Pages 244–266 in *Politics in Leadership: A Comparative Perspective*, edited by William A. Shack and Percy S. Cohen. Oxford: Clarendon Press.

Wyden, Peter
1962   *Suburbia's Coddled Kids.* Garden City: Doubleday.

Index

Printed in the United Kingdom
by Lightning Source UK Ltd.
126980UK00001B/40/A